MOOD TIDES

DIVINE PURPOSE IN THE RHYTHMS OF LIFE

Ronald Horton

JOURNEYFORTH

Greenville, South Carolina

Library of Congress Cataloging-in-Publication Data

Horton, Ronald Arthur, 1936-
  Mood tides : divine purpose in the rhythms of life / Ronald Horton.
    p. cm.
  Summary: "This book argues for the innocence of mood variations
so that they can be understood as purposed by God for our good and
His"—Provided by publisher.
  ISBN-13: 978-1-59166-780-3 (perfect bound pbk. : alk. paper)
  1. Emotions—Religious aspects—Christianity. I. Title.
  BV4597.3.H67 2008
  233'.5—dc22

                                                                2007038926

Cover Photo Credit: Rick Hyman, iStock

The fact that materials produced by other publishers may be referred
to in this volume does not constitute an endorsement of the content or
theological position of materials produced by such publishers.

All Scripture is quoted from the Authorized King James Version unless
otherwise noted.

NASB: Scripture taken from the NEW AMERICAN STANDARD
BIBLE®, Copyright © 1960, 1962, 1963, 1968, 1971, 1972, 1973, 1975,
1977, 1995 by The Lockman Foundation. Used by permission.

Mood Tides: Divine Purpose in the Rhythms of Life
Ronald Horton, PhD

Design by Elly Kalagayan
Page layout by Kelley Moore

© 2008 by BJU Press
Greenville, South Carolina 29614
JourneyForth is a division of BJU Press

ISBN 978-1-59166-780-3

15   14   13   12   11   10   9   8   7   6   5   4   3   2   1

To
Walter and Trudy
Fremont

Fair weather cometh out of the north.

Job 37:22

God made us moody,
not for defeat but for victory,
so that Jesus Christ's name
might be glorified.

Walter Fremont

CONTENTS

INTRODUCTION

In the day of prosperity be joyful, but in the day of adversity consider.

Ecclesiastes 7:14

MOURNING AND MIRTH

Solomon takes a serious line in Ecclesiastes 7. He opens with the dismal thought that "the day of death is better than the day of one's birth." He goes on to say, "It is better to go to the house of mourning, than to go to the house of feasting." It is better because a scene of grieving tends to serious thoughts and learning. Feasting, on the other hand, is the setting of folly. "The heart of fools is in the house of mirth." Wise words indeed from the wisest of men, words reinforced by common observation, but are we being urged to think always on the dark side of life?

Two chapters later, Solomon advocates enjoying the physical good that comes to us in the normal course of our earth-dwelling existence. "Go thy way, eat thy bread with joy, and drink thy wine with a merry heart; for God now accepteth thy works. Let thy garments be always white; and let thy head lack no ointment. Live joyfully with the wife whom thou lovest all the days of . . . thy vanity: . . . for that is thy portion in this life, and in thy labour which thou takest under the sun" (9:7–9).

How can Solomon affirm mirth after having devalued it in the passage on mourning? It does seem clear he is not speaking facetiously in the latter passage, for enjoying what life brings is a theme in his other writings also. We may conclude that both passages are divinely inspired truth—that Solomon is setting down a norm of minimal earthly good. His point is that life contains lows and highs, what disappoints and what gratifies, and that both "houses" are to be accepted as good and made use of. I am using these passages to spring some observations on what I will call "the rhythms of life."

These observations will take the form of an extended argument for the wise hand of God in our emotional lives. Lest as Joseph warned his brothers you "fall out by the way" before you have finished the journey, I will comment on the early terrain. The first section, "The Rhythms of Life," sets out the question to be addressed and indicates the position I will take on it. The next section, "Simplified Selves," is site preparation for what will follow. In this section chapters 3 through 5 treat misperceptions that stand in the path of my argument. Chapter 6 targets a model of the self mistakenly adopted by conservatives reacting to secular premises of the mental health field. The entire section may be skipped if the problems it addresses are of little interest and seem unimportant. Like a paper dragon, it won't hurt you if you leave it alone.

The book is not a formal account of its subject. Nor is it a personal meditation, though I write from some experience in the subject it treats. It aims to identify some simple truths God has provided for the encouragement of His people. That is the task before us, and to that we now turn.

THE RHYTHMS OF LIFE

While the earth remaineth, seedtime and harvest, and cold and heat, and summer and winter, and day and night shall not cease.

Genesis 8:22

1

PEAKS AND VALLEYS

What I am calling the rhythms of life refers on the more obvious level to the flow of the pleasant and the unpleasant that seems to persist in our lives. Of the two it is the unpleasant especially that gives us a sense of the alternation of good and bad we connect with earthly life. Good times lull us into a false sense of normality. We hardly recognize their presence until they end. We then rack our brains to understand how and why the bad times have come. Later from a distance we are able to see the pleasant and unpleasant appearing in more or less continuous succession.

Justifying the bad in life has been a continuing challenge for thinkers who specialize in such questions but also for people like ourselves. Yes, we live in a fallen world. But why this particular pain has come into my particular life at this particular time is finally a mystery. God rules. His mind is unsearchable and His ways past finding out. Most likely the painful situation came for a dozen major reasons and for fifty thousand lesser reasons that only God can keep track of and blend together in a way that makes perfect sense. Sometimes God puts His finger on the cause of our pain, when it is of our own making, so we can avoid it in the future. Sometimes He allows us to see that the loss of one good has been necessary to our gaining of a greater, more enduring good. But it should be enough for us to trust that "his way is perfect" and to have faith with David that He "maketh my way perfect" (Ps. 18:30, 32).

Still, both Scripture and common observation suggest that usually, human nature being what it is, character grows better in bad times than in good. Bad times open minds to unwelcome truths—truths to which they are closed when life seems going well. "Sweet are the uses of adversity," says Shakespeare's duke, forced into the forest by his usurping brother.[1] The duke's present low condition is prompting him to improve his life—the part of his life that especially counts. He will rule his banished court in kindness and moral wisdom. He will not let his time of deprivation go to waste. Low conditions, says the duke, are times to ponder one's mortality.

There is another evident reason that bad times come. The world would be much poorer if Christlikeness were limited only to imitating the pleasant times in the life of the Savior. The world needs examples of Christians holding steady in times of stress. It needs to see that the new life in Christ holds up in foul weather as well as in fair, that it can flourish during times when false life-views founder. Dark times identify the genuine. "They breathe truth," declares Shakespeare's dying duke of Lancaster, "that breathe their words in pain."[2]

Yet another reason with strong biblical warrant is that times of difficulty for the Christian call forth special spiritual exertions that yield special benefits. Like resistance training in athletics, these exertions firm the character to accomplish greater work for God. "Tribulation worketh patience," wrote Paul, a man much subject to it, and patience is a major theme in his epistles (Rom. 5:3).

But that is not all. Bad times also provide occasions for the accumulation of that heavenly treasure Jesus urged His disciples to lay up for themselves in Matthew 6:20. The unpressured Christian would be poorer in the next world for having had no trials in this one. For these reasons and no doubt others, there does seem to be a wavelike rhythm in life in which peaks are followed by valleys and valleys by peaks in measured and merciful intervals.

However, by rhythms I refer also to the shifting states of the interior life, to the emotional fluctuations that produce good or ill thoughts of ourselves and our lives—thoughts that may or may not be tied to our circumstances. Most of us would, I think, agree that there is a rough alternation of elevated and subdued spirits that enlivens and dampens our appetite for activity and our enthusiasms for the enjoyments about us. On one day we feel an eagerness to apply ourselves to the day's duties; on another day we must rely on force of habit and conviction to meet our responsibilities. On one day a minor success—in business, in sports, in academics, in social recognition—can seem a major one; on another day, a major success can seem a minor one, or pass almost unnoticed. The same facts get framed diversely depending on the day.

Emotional highs and lows are certainly instigated by circumstances—by pleasant and unpleasant situations and events—but the point here is that they occur also in the absence of external promptings. They can just come. For some they are severe. What is for one person a momentary case of the blues can constitute for another a considerable emotional challenge. What is for many a mild euphoria can be for others a giddy high almost as disconcerting as a period of dejection.

Much has been written about emotional *bipolarity*, in which the sufferer experiences emotional highs and lows of unusual severity or duration. Simple remedies are sometimes glibly proposed by theorists who have not themselves been afflicted in this way and have not felt the daily burden of calming and buoying the spirits of loved ones coping with these debilitating extremes. For most of us, the onset of low and high feelings is as difficult to explain as anything can be in the human world. Emotions have a way of marching to the beat of their own drummer. Indeed, I will maintain, the drummer may be divine.

2

DIVINE PURPOSE

I am proposing an idea that may seem so obvious some will say to themselves, "Why should I bother to read on about something so evident and trite as this?" Others may find it so strange as to ask, "Where did *that* notion come from?" The idea is that God purposes high and low spirits. I will contend that both high and low spirits have their place in the spiritual life and that, contrary to common belief, neither is a sure sign of spiritual victory or defeat.

God ordained seasons of high and low spirits in Israel in the annual feasts. The autumn harvest festival began with a day of low spirits, of atonement, when every Israelite was to afflict his spirit, thinking on his sins. Following close on the day of low spirits was the Feast of Tabernacles, during which the Israelites were commanded to show grateful exuberant joy. It should not therefore be surprising that God provides periodic occasions for low as well as high spirits in individual lives.

God indeed authorizes emotional shifts in response to the shifting circumstances of life. Jesus defended high spirits when He was asked by the scribes and Pharisees why His disciples "eat and drink"—that is "feast"—after Matthew's dinner. He replied they had good reason to enjoy the moment. The Bridegroom was now with them. Later, He said, there would be a time to mourn. His disciples would fast when the Bridegroom was taken away (Matt. 9:9–15).

That God authorizes unprompted mood swings is a more radical proposal. I believe that emotional highs and lows are structured into us by our Creator for reasons we do not totally understand. There may well be a therapeutic benefit in low spirits, something purgative as in the downside of the business cycle. There may be a restorative effect in high spirits having something to do with endurance in a fallen world. It is said that a horse being ridden or driven on a road with moderate grades and descents can last longer than one traversing a completely level stretch. The inclines and declines call into play different combinations of muscles, allowing them intermittent rest.

Scripture does not require us to suppress these emotional states but asks us rather to make good use of them. I suspect that apart from emotional lows some would never entertain serious thoughts. Certainly apart from emotional highs it is difficult for the spirit to rise in praise. "Is any among you afflicted? let him pray. Is any merry? let him sing," commands James (James 5:13). Notice that this injunction does not propose correctives to these emotional states. James is not saying jerk yourselves out of these moods. He is telling us what to be doing while we are in them. We would likely counsel the opposite. "Are your spirits soaring today? You had better pray. Are they sinking? Try singing. Tone down your hilarity; throw off your sadness. These are aberrations." James is supported by Paul, who tells the Romans to rejoice with those who rejoice and to weep with those who weep (Rom. 12:15). He did not question the appropriateness of these emotional states.

Divine Purpose

Emotional fluctuation varies from person to person. Some have wider and longer swings than others. Some have an emotional life pitched higher than the usual, others lower, still others settled pretty much in the middle. Some have feelings constantly in motion. Others have long plateaus or vary little. Our God loves diversity, and He has different labors for His very different human creatures to do. These labors can vary in cost and pain.

But if emotional variation is inevitable, spiritual variation is not. Satan delights to attack us at the extremes of our emotional cycles as well as at seasons of life that push us up or down. He need not succeed. We can resist him better if we understand that it is not the extremes themselves but what we do with them that brings about spiritual victory or defeat. We can condemn their indulgent states, pride and despair, without condemning the fluctuations themselves.

For elation and depression are normal moods intended for good. They are moods, it is true, which some must endure as acute and chronic infirmities. Yet they may be endured like other infirmities with the assurance that God can turn suffering to positive gain. There is divine purpose in the rhythms of life.

Simplified Selves

What therefore God hath joined together, let not man put asunder.

Matthew 19:6

3

A Difficulty

My direction of thought on emotional states puts me at odds with certain preconceptions about the emotional life. The first is that up is good and down is bad. This preconception targets depression. The second is that down is good and up is bad. This targets elation, particularly in the form of self-esteem. These no doubt combine into a third preconception that requires the avoidance of both up and down—that is, the maintaining of an unflappable evenness of mood. In this view all divergences from a normal emotional state are undesirable and unnecessary.

I propose that all these preconceptions are wrong and seriously so—that they are at variance with common observation and with Scripture. I will mostly leave the evidence from common observation to speak for itself and draw my support from Scripture. I will do so in some detail because these preconceptions are deeply rooted in present-day thinking.

They are rooted also in certain stoutly maintained theological emphases. To argue that both up and down are good—willed of God, purposive and beneficial—will bring us into controversial territory. We will need to consider the meaning of biblical selfhood. We will need to give thought also to how the natural and the supernatural meet in Christian experience. These subjects, though not basic to our faith, are bedrock to the issues being raised in these pages and need addressing early before receiving extended treatment later.

When we allow that emotional highs and lows are in themselves natural and good, we find ourselves in the position of allowing mind states that some Christian specialists in these matters disapprove on biblical grounds. Because secular psychology has removed moral responsibility from the emotional life, some Christian psychologists have felt it necessary to insist on total spiritual sovereignty over the feelings. Total spiritual sovereignty over the feelings implies that emotional states are rooted in spiritual attitudes. If so, the troublesome ones must be spiritually correctable and need not continue. If they need not continue, they are indulgent states that indicate spiritual failure. A Christian who suffers from acute recurring low spirits, for example, is sinning from failing to draw on his spiritual resources.

Consequently natural causes of emotional disorders get downgraded in importance, if not indeed disallowed, and natural remedies are dismissed as palliatives treating only symptoms. Raising one's self-estimate, a commonly prescribed corrective to low feelings, is especially targeted by this view as promoting pride, the grand enemy of spiritual character. To regard self-esteem in a positive way is to deny man's moral worthlessness. To advise natural remedies for low feelings (exercise, medication, social interaction, improved sleep habits) is, by this reasoning, to question the power of God to order the redeemed mind. It is also to become complicit in the sufferer's spiritual defeat.

Those who reject natural causes and remedies of emotional disorders on spiritual grounds do so from two premises with which every Christian must agree. The first is that spiritual resources—Scripture, prayer, Christian fellowship, godly advice—are sufficient for spiritual living. The second, which logically follows, is that there is no excuse for spiritual defeat. The truth of these is beyond question. It is absolutely certain, and necessary to be maintained, that believers have been given, in Peter's words, "all things that pertain unto life and godliness, through the knowledge of him that hath called us to glory and virtue" (2 Pet. 1:3). To deny the sufficiency of the believer's spiritual resources for spiritual health puts us in conflict with plain Scripture. It also raises questions about the providence of a God Who, we must believe, has provided the means for obedience to what He commands.

The real question, however, is not the sufficiency of spiritual resources for spiritual health but whether spiritual health entirely embraces emotional health and controls it. We have all encountered a spiritually prospering, mature Christian who has experienced protracted physical suffering. It would seem to follow that whereas some physical suffering has spiritual causes, not all does. Jesus was asked by His disciples, "Who did sin, this man, or his parents, that he was born blind?" Jesus replied, "Neither hath this man sinned, nor his parents: but that the works of God should be made manifest in him" (John 9:2–3). Paul begged God three times to remove a physical infirmity but was made to understand that God willed the infirmity to remain for two reasons: to defeat pride of spiritual knowledge and to show His sustaining strength. "My grace is sufficient for thee: for my strength is made perfect in weakness" (2 Cor. 12:9). So it must be that physical illness can occur as an occasion to reveal the power and goodness of God and to restrain wrong tendencies. May it not be true also of emotional suffering that whereas some has moral causes, not all does? Might not emotional as well as physical pain be innocent and productive of good?

The question is important. If spiritual resources are sufficient to rule all that belongs to the spiritual domain, and the spiritual domain is deemed to include all mental functions including the emotional, mere brain activity cannot be a consequential factor in the emotional life. Emotional instabilities such as mania and depression are entirely on the spiritual side of the divide in this dichotomy and become spiritual phenomena subject to spiritual control, aberrations of the spiritual life. They are not to be regarded as natural disorders treatable by natural means.

This position raises questions for those of us who have observed in our pets just about the full range of emotions we have seen in ourselves. Dogs and cats, for instance, experience anger, jealousy, grief, insecurity, desire for food and companionship. Zoo animals in close confinement can show symptoms of depression. Lest we doubt our inferences from observation, we may justifiably conclude from Scripture that Balaam's donkey had some sort of emotional life. The miracle consisted in supplying language to what already existed in the donkey's mind. And yet animals obviously cannot be said to have a spiritual life.

It seems inconsistent to deny to humans a physically grounded emotional life we allow to animals. If the entire immaterial nature of man, his entire mental life, is in the domain of the spiritual, how do we account for the evident fact that animals have some of it? Would it not be simpler to conclude that our capacity for emotional experience, adverse and extreme as well as agreeable and mild, is part of our natural humanity—a humanity which, though affected by inherited sin, God has fashioned for His glory and our good?

4

A RELATED DIFFICULTY

If such is the case, that emotional variations are an innocent function of our nature, we then run into another difficulty. The biblical thinker has an ingrained suspicion of things natural, as indeed he should. He knows that "the natural man receiveth not the things of the Spirit of God: for they are foolishness unto him: neither can he know them, because they are spiritually discerned" (1 Cor. 2:14). The natural man in Scripture is spiritually blind and morally corrupt, driven by carnal desires, caught up in his own purposes and importance. The opposite of the natural is the spiritual, the perceptions and desires of regenerated man, whose entire being and course of life express the God-life within him.

On the other hand, we are given to understand elsewhere in Scripture that the natural is approved of God whereas the unnatural is disapproved. Paul writes of reprobate persons who lack natural affection (Rom. 1:31; 2 Tim. 3:3), some of whom in their depravity even "did change the natural use into that which is against nature" (Rom. 1:26). He reminds the Corinthians that nature teaches men the shamefulness of their having long hair (1 Cor. 11:14). Parents should "train up a child in the way he should go," in line with his natural bent, according to the better reading of the inspired proverb (Prov. 22:6). The child's natural bent in this instance is not his inherited disposition to sin but his created capacities and inclinations. When we speak of a person's finding a line of work that is natural to him, we are using *natural* in this general and positive sense. In such instances as these, the opposite of the natural is not the spiritual, what aligns with the true, but the deviational, what goes awry from its purpose. Can it be then that the natural is both bad and good?

We have encountered a paradox, a two-sided truth. Reformation thinkers centered on the condition of the sinner in justification as morally worthless and on the inherited nature as thoroughly corrupt. They disallowed personal righteousness, in keeping with the theological fault lines between them and their Roman Catholic opponents. What can get underemphasized, if not overlooked, is the other side of the Bible's teaching about redeemed humanity. It is of course outrageous to speak of the moral worth of unregenerate sinners, which we all either are or were. It is also outrageous to deny worth to the object of God's re-created work—redeemed man, who is being refashioned according to the Creator's original intention. Concerning personal righteousness, Paul in the first eleven chapters of Romans argues with devastating thoroughness there is no such thing. In the remaining five chapters he insists there had better be. The Roman Christians were far from perfect; they needed instruction and correction. But Paul nonetheless was "persuaded . . . that ye also are full of goodness" (15:14). Personal righteousness is both an absolute impossibility and an absolute necessity.

The solution to the paradox is, of course, the ability of redeemed man, supported by divine grace, to conform to the character and works of God. The believer's sanctification is part of the grand program of God to restore His creation from its fallen condition. Redeemed man is doubly the handiwork of God, fashioned unflawed in the original creation and refashioned in redemption. God is working in our natures what He approves as honorable and good, a renewing of that which He pronounced "very good" on the sixth day of creation and into which He breathed something of His own nature. We must ascribe goodness and value to the redeemed self.

There is, furthermore, immeasurable value, if only latent and potential, in the being of every person ever born. God ascribed value to all that He created in the six days of His creative work, including the most notable of his works for which He fashioned the rest. "Every creature [created thing] of God is good," said Paul, referring not only to the prefallen world (1 Tim. 4:4). This value is fully realized as God perfects His creative work in the character of the believer. Both redeemed and unredeemed must respect their declared value as greater than that of "the whole world" (Mark 8:36).

We hold simultaneously then to the utter moral worthlessness of the inherited nature and to the measureless worth of the created nature restored in regenerated man. We also hold to the value of the created nature residual and normative in all mankind. We must value those things about us that have been placed in us by God, whether originally in creation or interventionally in redemption, while denying value to the unredeemed part of us—to "my flesh," that is, wherein "dwelleth no good thing" (Rom. 7:18). "How much then is a man better than a sheep?" asked the Lord rhetorically of His disciples (Matt. 12:12). Speaking in understatement He assured them, "Ye are of more value than many sparrows" (10:31). Who would be so bold as to dispute the Lord?

5

Two Cautions

Once we recognize the importance of our natural created being, we need not degrade natural remedies for treating problems of the emotional life. God approves of natural means. He created them. He commonly uses them to answer our prayers. When Jesus raised to life Jairus's daughter, supernatural and natural conjoined in her full restoration. He told her to arise and then "commanded that something should be given her to eat" (Mark 5:43). Here the supernatural came powerfully into play in the restoring of life, but it did not invalidate the natural. The girl needed food. May it not also be the case that when God is meeting needs of the emotional life affected by physical conditions He can be working through natural as well as spiritual means?

In arguing this point in the chapters that follow, I will try to avoid two self-defeating tendencies in biblical controversy. They drive conscientious advocates of biblical truth to extremes—extremes that caricature positions they mean to defend and leave confusion among those they mean to help.

Responses to dangerous religious or secular ideas can all too easily get skewed in an aggressive effort to counter thoroughly the targeted error. As a result, God's people are left with a partial, misshapen account of the truth they sorely need—better off, no doubt, than they were without it, but still poorly equipped and unsettled.

The first tendency is the habit of not recognizing more than one side of a two-sided truth.

The common term for a two-sided truth is *paradox*, ordinarily defined as "a seeming contradiction." We have met paradox already in the double sense of *nature* in Scripture: the natural self is both bad and good, depending on what is meant by it. Here as elsewhere in biblical paradox, the truth is not at odds with itself. We are presented with a *seeming* contradiction. Scripture warns against the bondage of the inherited self, a sinful legacy from Adam, aggravated by Satan and at war with the spiritual powers and potentials in redeemed man. But Scripture also affirms the goodness of the created self, both the thoughts and behaviors still normative for man after the fall and those we progress toward after the new birth. It is a sin to bend toward the inherited nature; it is a sin not to bend toward the created nature. The goodness of nature therefore must be both denied and affirmed. The method of this seeming contradiction is to lead us, in the process of resolving it, to a valuable insight, formulating a truth for ourselves in a richly memorable way.

Paradoxes test the patience of readers, including exegetes of Scripture where paradoxes are not at all infrequent. A paradox can be a manner of expressing something that itself is not difficult to comprehend. When Jesus told His disciples that the wide gate opens toward destruction and the narrow gate toward life, the contradiction was simply between the factual truth and their ingrained way of thinking, between reality and appearance. To resolve the paradox required only relinquishing a misperception, replacing ignorance with knowledge. The paradox was simply an arresting pictorial packaging of a truth.

But when Jesus, describing His death, spoke of the need for a grain of wheat to fall into the ground and die in order to produce new life, the apparent contradiction was in the very nature of the truth itself—indeed in the actual structure of the reality being represented. The idea that death must precede life is a startling truth, observable in nature but darkly mysterious as a universal principle—one that operates in both physical and spiritual domains. It requires special explanation in order to be understood. Paradoxes, that is, can be merely verbal mechanisms, such as that of the two gates, or they can be of the actual substance of the idea, such as that of the grain of wheat. The latter further divide into the easily resolvable or the ultimately unresolvable. The unresolvable include some of the most important truths we have.

When we fail to embrace both sides of a biblical paradox—that is, two truths in apparent conflict, both of which are affirmed in Scripture—we engage in doctrinal nullification. However high the motive, the effect can be disastrous when one truth is lost for the sake of another. Satan delights to set in competition truths both of which we greatly need.

Arguments in defense of truth go awry also because of a second tendency: reactional thinking. Conservative thinking on the emotional life has generally taken shape as a direct response to the work of the Austrian psychiatrist Sigmund Freud. It is easy in controversy to forget that a position held by an enemy of biblical truth such as Freud need not be in every respect wrong.

Freud set out to map the unconscious self and did it in a way that weakens moral responsibility. We may reject the Freudian unconscious without denying the existence of the unconscious it-self. Freud was not the first to propose that there are depths in the human mind. The idea is prominent in Plato. It is everywhere in Scripture itself. "The spirit of man is the candle of the Lord," search-ing all his innermost parts (Prov. 20:27). God knows our thoughts and purposes "afar off"—before we ourselves are even aware of them (Ps. 139:2). The brain is a multitasking marvel, and beyond that is the mysterious interplay of its synapses and the soul.

Again, Freud's conflict model of the personality, of the sensual against the rational and moral, was not the first to appear in intel-lectual history. The concept of continuous psychic struggle is old as humankind. Paul gave us a picture of the redeemed mind in which the old and new natures are continually at war. "The flesh lusteth against the Spirit, and the Spirit against the flesh: and these are contrary the one to the other: so that ye cannot do the things that ye would" (Gal. 5:17). The difference is that in the Freudian model a subverting potency is given to the depths and the flesh as ultimate determinants of behavior whereas in the biblical model the new nature and its animating principle can dominate and will ultimately prevail.

Still again, rejecting Freud does not require denigrating the feel-ings. Both emotional and rational powers have been infected by sin in fallen man, and both serve man well in his regenerated con-dition. Jonathan Edwards said it well:

> Such is man's nature, that he is very inactive, any otherwise
> than he is influenced by either *love* or *hatred, desire, hope, fear,*
> or some other affection. These affections we see to be the mov-
> ing springs in all the affairs of life, which engage men in all
> their pursuits; and especially in all affairs wherein they are ear-
> nestly engaged, and which they pursue with vigour. . . . Take

away all *love* and *hatred*, all *hope* and *fear*, all *anger, zeal,* and affectionate *desire,* and the world would be, in a great measure, motionless and dead.

In fact, says Edwards, "the Holy Scriptures every where place religion very much in the affections; such as fear, hope, love, hatred, desire, joy, sorrow, gratitude, compassion, and zeal. In a word, there never was any thing *considerable* brought to pass in the heart or life of any man living, by the things of religion, that had not his heart *deeply affected* by those things"[1] (italics mine). *Heart* here has its modern meaning as the seat of the emotions.

Reactional thinking is a special danger in serious controversy. Instead of forming a position directly from Scripture, the zealous Christian advocate may stake out his position diametrically opposite the erroneous one, forgetting that error is not always 180 degrees from the truth. Error may lie 90 degrees off the truth or even be sitting on truth's borders. If truth, let us say, is north by the compass, error is not always due south; it may be east or west, even northwest, and even in not-so-rare instances north-northwest.

To be in accord with divinely revealed truth, our positions must be formed naturally from Scripture, not counterrelationally to what Scripture opposes. Otherwise, in reacting to a position that is mostly wrong but partially right we may find ourselves proposing one that is mostly right but partially wrong, a reverse image of the one opposed and both inaccurate. How useless would be a weathervane whose base pivoted with it, turning in its entirety to face the wind, so that north showed always opposite to the way the wind was blowing.

6

MISLEADING MODELS

Nowhere is reactive thinking more consequential than in our theorizing about the human self. Whole worldviews have rested on concepts of the self, justifying life attitudes, establishing values, and providing rationales for behavior. For Christians a true view of the self is second in importance only to a true view of God.

Ideas of the self determine views of emotional experience. Today's ideas of the self come to us from the ancient past in two traditions. Behind the Freudian idea of the self with the rational ego, the lusting and conniving id, and the censoring superego are the great Greek models of Plato and Aristotle. Plato described a three-part soul with reason ruling, though with difficulty, over the emotions, which need constant subjugation. He divided the emotional nature into the "spirited" part containing anger and the less noble part containing the appetites. Anger can be harnessed to virtue whereas the sexual urge always opposes it, he said.

Aristotle followed the same divisions, analyzing the soul into ascending powers in which reason presides over the rest. Though he gave more value than Plato to the emotions, he likewise regarded the soul's health as dependent on reason's rule. Since both philosophers' accounts of the faculties have to do with the proper conduct of life, both may be regarded as moral models of the self.

Freud's analysis of the personality is strikingly similar to the model he inherited from the Greeks. The components are much the same. The rational faculty, Freud's ego, must govern for the health of the personality. But it is not the vital center. The primal agent of behavior is the libido of the sensual id, ever seeking its gratification. It must be held in bounds. And yet holding the id within bounds produces pathological mind states and behavior. Plato's ideal of the soul's health and Aristotle's hierarchy of the faculties are shadowed in Freud, but the relations of the parts have been altered into a new dynamic.

Freud also made what had been called the conscience a social construct, formed by parental and other environmental influences, rather than an innate sense of right and wrong. As a censoring moral agent, the superego, as he named it, is a repressor of natural urges. Traditional moralists condemned Freudian theory for encouraging sexual license. They rightly regarded it as a threat to the moral life and saw it driving the sexual revolution of the sixties.

Freud's account became inscribed in modern culture as a revolutionary alternative to traditional thought. The Freudian model complicated behavior to the point that moral responsibility was difficult to assess, placing the source of behavior beneath conscious thought, ascertainable only by psychoanalysis. And yet Freud's description of the self was very much itself a moral model. It implied a standard of behavior to be regarded as natural and normal. It was squarely in the classical tradition of the moral self while making moral control problematical.

By the middle of the twentieth century the Freudian moral model was being replaced by a medical model of the self. This model too has antecedents in the ancient past. In this tradition, emotional temperament is rooted physically in the balance of fluids basic to life. In the Roman era, the Greek physician Galen (c. 130–c. 200) proposed a concept of the self in which health, temperament, and behavior are determined by the balancing of four body "humors." An excess of red bile, or blood, produces the sanguine temperament and associated behavior; of black bile, the melancholic; of yellow bile, the choleric; and of phlegm, the phlegmatic. Though Galen did not himself deny the immaterial nature of man—he held with Plato concerning the soul—his work could be understood to support a materialist view of the self.

In medieval theory the Galenic humors are affected by the positions of the stars at any given time but particularly at one's birth. So it is, for example, that a person whose nature was choleric by the accident of his birth must be particularly careful of his behavior when the planet Mars is in ascendancy or he could be undone by his anger. The practice of medicine was conducted in close connection with astrology, for zodiacal considerations must combine with biological for accurate diagnosis and remediation. The resulting model was materialist and determinist with a small role for reason and will.

With the rise of science in the seventeenth century, especially after William Harvey's discovery of the circulation of the blood in 1628, Galen's medical model was displaced by an improved account of human physiology. It enhanced the health of European man but could also serve a materialist view of the self. Plato's moral model of the soul, buttressed by Aristotle's hierarchical divisions of the faculties, was not eclipsed, being largely taken for granted until the late eighteenth century when it came under relentless attack from Rousseau (1712–78) and the rising Romantic movement. Both models, the moral and the medical, remained influential in secular thought, though the moral less so as the twentieth century wore on.

Today in applied psychology censorable behavior is more likely to be attributed to erratic brain activity than to a misshapen emotional past. Freudian psychoanalysis has been largely displaced by physical therapies, particularly medication. An array of drugs is available to regulate depression and subdue agitation. As in the Galenic medical model, personality disorders require the moderation of abnormal chemical activity, though it is hormones rather than humors that must be kept in balance. On the theoretical side, cognitive psychology has come to the fore, tying errant behaviors to inaccurate thinking resulting from faulty brain circuitry on the analogy of computer intelligence. For today's professionals, mental health is almost entirely a physical matter.

Conservative responses to the Freudian and more recent materialist models of the self have been rapid and vigorous. Both the moral model of Freud and the materialist models of today's psychology agree in virtually eliminating moral responsibility. Both are determinist, attributing moral behavior to agents other than conscious thought and will. Both deny the spiritual side of human existence. Therefore both are inevitably rejected by moral conservatives. No account of the self that weakens moral responsibility is acceptable to those who regard accountability to God as the primary issue in life.

In response to these secular ideas of the self, conservatives have reinstated Plato's moral model, with rational judgment requiring suppression of the passions, which are associated with the flesh. The conscience has been restored as not just a social construct but fundamentally the inborn moral law of God. Human nature is held to be dichotomous, divided between the physical and the mental, the former being the province of medical science, the latter the province of spiritual care. This reactional idea of the self is closer to Scripture than those it opposes but still seriously flawed. It is responsible for a view of the emotions that stands in the way of positive insights from God's Word.

There is another regrettable outcome. Secularist models of the self have their day and then cease to be taken seriously—by anyone, that is, except invested critics who oppose them. Freudian theory has been losing ground in the academic and professional world for fifty years. Freudian psychoanalysis, with its strange entities of ego, superego, and id, has seemed increasingly quaint and archaic— "medieval" in the words of one critic. It no longer has a place in psychological research. A result is that conservative theorists lose credibility when they retain their counter-Freudian model unaware that their enemy has abandoned his campsite for another.

A common flaw in secular models of the self and conservative responses to them is their simplification of what must remain ultimately a mystery: the God-created human self. To simplify truth about the self is not in itself wrong. Humans simplify when organizing important areas of their experience to bring them under control. Analyzing the self into an ordered arrangement of distinct agencies continues to serve a purpose in moral instruction, keeping desires subordinate to reason in judgments requiring deliberation.

But the model of the mind invoked for that purpose should not be mistaken for the entity it represents. For a more satisfactory view of the self we must turn to the ultimate source of what is to be known about ourselves, the Word of God.

The Mysterious Self

I will praise thee; for I am fearfully and wonderfully made: marvellous are thy works; and that my soul knoweth right well.

Psalm 139:14

7

INTERWOVEN POWERS

Where we Christians must go for our concept of the self is to Scripture. What can be frustrating is that Scripture provides no simple schematic account of the self. When we turn to passages treating the agents of thought and feeling and the resultant actions, we find no tidy set of mental components and functions as in the great classical models and their modern variations. In the Western moral tradition, head must control heart, reason must master passion, at least in most matters; but this psychological split is not characteristic of Eastern thought, nor is it found in Scripture.

We need not look far in a standard biblical encyclopedia to discover that expressions referring to the self in Scripture do not cohere into a structure anything like that of the classical models. The variable, overlapping, and often synonymous uses of *soul*, *spirit*, *heart*, *mind*, and *man* do not reveal levels of the faculties, much less a scheme that Plato or Aristotle would recognize.

In fact, mind as a concept familiar to the Greek world is scarcely in view in the Old Testament or even in much of the New. Where it does appear in Paul's epistles, it blends with the Hebrew *heart*. To possess "the mind of Christ" (1 Cor. 2:16) is to possess both much less and much more than the factual mental content and intellectual powers of the Son of God. Obviously our possessible portion of this mind is less, for no finite creature can presume to know the mind of Him Whose thoughts are not our thoughts and Whose ways are past finding out. Nor can man's mental equipment compare with his Creator's.

The "mind of Christ" is then clearly less than the divine powers of cognition. But it is also more. The expression speaks of submission to the will of the Father, a matter of will and heart extending well beyond mere reasoning. It speaks of the bridling of purposes, "bringing into captivity every thought to the obedience of Christ" (2 Cor. 10:5). Contrasting with the mind of Christ is the "froward heart" of Proverbs 11:20, the prideful heart of Psalm 101:5 and Proverbs 16:5, and the sin-hardened heart of Psalm 95:8. As a New Testament concept, mind designates not a mental faculty but the inner purposing part of us. To possess the "mind of Christ" is to share, as it were, His life stance and values, more than a fund of knowledge and a reasoning apparatus.

Heart in Scripture, when it does not refer to the physical organ or to emotional strength as in courage (Ps. 40:12; cf. "spirit" in Ps. 143:7), indicates the self's deep center—the hidden ultimate source of all that may be observed about a person. Out of the heart "are the issues [issuings forth] of life" (Prov. 4:23). Among these outflowings of the heart are thoughts, feelings, desires, inclinations, and determinations. Conscience is there. After David had cut off part of the robe of the sleeping King Saul, his "heart smote him" (1 Sam. 24:5). Heart is the inner essential person in emphatic distinction from the outer apparent person. "Man looketh on the outward appearance, but the Lord looketh on the heart" (1 Sam. 16:7). As a man "thinketh in his heart, so is he" (Prov. 23:7). Just to "confess with thy mouth the Lord Jesus" is not enough for salvation. It is necessary to "believe in thine heart" what has been publicly declared (Rom. 10:9–10).

The heart is the center and source of the moral life, for out of it "proceed evil thoughts, murders, adulteries, fornications, thefts, false witness, blasphemies" (Matt. 15:19). It is "deceitful above all things, and desperately wicked" (Jer. 17:9). From the heart thoughts arise (Luke 24:38), and in the heart reasoning occurs (Luke 5:22). God probes the heart (Rom. 8:27) and ponders it (Prov. 21:2). He knows "the hearts of all men" (Acts 1:24). The heart is known only to God (1 Kings 8:39).

The Hebrew and Greek words for *soul* (OT *nephesh*, NT *psyche*) have comparable ranges of meaning. Both can simply indicate physical life (Exod. 21:23; John 10:15; Acts 15:26). Both can refer merely to physical persons (Exod. 1:5; Acts 7:14; 27:37). Soul pertains to the physical side of the self in Isaiah 58, when among the conditions for God's blessing are that one "draw out thy soul to the hungry, and satisfy the afflicted soul," after which "the Lord shall . . . satisfy thy soul in drought" (vv. 10–11).

But soul typically refers to the inner essential person as he appears to God. "The soul that sinneth, it shall die," says the Lord through the prophet Ezekiel (18:4, 20), quite evidently referring to more than just the end of the body. The rich man of Luke 12:19 speaks to a self he foolishly conceives in mere physical terms: "Soul, thou hast much goods laid up for many years." God responds with a more adequate view of the soul: "Fool, this night thy soul shall be required of thee."

The same Greek word (*psyche*) can be translated both "soul" and "life," and so it is in Mark 8. Jesus tells His disciples, "Whosoever will come after me, let him deny himself, and take up his cross, and follow me. For whosoever will save his life [*psyche*] shall lose it; but whosoever shall lose his life [*psyche*] for my sake and the gospel's, the same shall save it. For what shall it profit a man, if he shall gain the whole world, and lose his own soul [*psyche*]? Or what shall a man give in exchange for his soul [*psyche*]?" (vv. 34–37). Notice that the loss of the self is represented on two levels—temporal physical loss ("lose his life for my sake and the gospel's") and eternal total loss ("lose his own soul")—and that *psyche* denotes both. Jesus told His disciples, "I lay down my life [*psyche*], that I might take it again" (John 10:17), referring obviously not to His inner essential nature.

The meaning of *soul* is further variable, often reflecting the particular aspect of personality with which its context is concerned. It can speak of an emotional state, especially of desire or fear. In Psalm 119 the soul "breaketh" from longing (v. 20), "melteth for heaviness" (v. 28), "fainteth" for deliverance (v. 81), and is continually in danger ("in my hand," v. 109). Similarly, "soul" in Matthew 26:38 ("My soul is exceeding sorrowful, even unto death") speaks of emotional vitality that can be crushed. In these senses it is close to "spirit" in 1 Corinthians 16:18 and 2 Corinthians 7:13, where Paul writes of the refreshing of a person's state of mind by another.

In both Hebrew and Greek, "spirit" (OT *ruah*, NT *pneuma*) has as a core meaning the idea of air and hence of wind or breathing. Like "soul" it speaks broadly of life in general. It is the vital animating element breathed into man by God (Zech. 12:1) that at death "shall return unto God who gave it" (Eccles. 12:7). Jesus cried, "Into thy hands I commend my spirit" (Luke 23:46). It can denote physical consciousness: concerning the Egyptian youth resuscitated by David's men it is said "his spirit came again to him" (1 Sam. 30:12). *Spirit* also designates the immaterial side of reality, which the Pharisees failed to understand (John 3:6–10) and the Sadducees denied (Acts 23:8). Contrasted with man's sin-corrupted nature, it denotes the God-life implanted in redeemed man that contends with the flesh (John 3:6; Gal. 5:16–25). Concretely *spirit* can refer to particular capacities or skills with which a person has been endowed by God for a purpose (Deut. 34:9; cf. 1 Cor. 12:1–30). Still again, *spirit* can refer to an emotional state needing moderation and control (Prov. 25:28). The spirit in this sense can be calmed. God pictures to His prophet the chariots of judgment that "have quieted my spirit in the north country" (Zech. 6:8). It can be used figuratively. Expressive of life breath in a hyperbolic sense, *spirit* can be arrested in stunned wonderment. When the queen of Sheba witnessed Solomon's wealth and wisdom, "there was no more spirit in her" (1 Kings 10:5).

Soul and *spirit* seem akin to *heart* in Mary's evocation of Hannah's prayer in the Magnificat. Whereas Hannah had exclaimed "My heart rejoiceth in the Lord" (1 Sam. 2:1), Mary prays, "My soul doth magnify the Lord, and my spirit hath rejoiced in God my Saviour" (Luke 1:46–47). It seems clear that Mary's "soul" and "spirit" are an instance of Hebrew poetical variation and therefore that all three words, including Hannah's "heart," have to do with the center of the self. Here *spirit* is something like the vital breath of the soul.

Similarly Paul's reference to "your whole spirit and soul and body" in 1 Thessalonians 5:23 seems not to intend a distinction between separate powers of spirit and soul but rather to convey inclusiveness, "spirit" connoting the frame of mind and "soul" the total inner man productive of it. (The same kind of cumulative series occurs in Mark 12:30, where Jesus, quoting Deuteronomy 6:5, enunciated "the first commandment of all" as the obligation to "love the Lord thy God with all thine heart, and with all thy soul, and with all thy mind, and with all thy strength.") Likewise in Hebrews 4:12 the penetrating action of the Word of God, "piercing even to the dividing asunder of soul and spirit," evidently does not indicate a division of soul from spirit, separating two distinct entities, but rather a single action: a slicing apart of the self with the exposing of its deepest recesses.

These recesses are not charted in Scripture. They remain mysterious, for God has not neatly packaged up the human self for our inspection. Where is that dream space in which "the angel of the Lord appeared unto [Joseph]" and reassured him about completing his marriage (Matt. 1:20)? Where do intimations come from? When Paul and his companions "assayed to go into Bithynia," through what mental agency did "the Spirit suffer them not" (Acts 16:7)? How indeed does the Spirit of God inhabit His earthly temples (1 Cor. 6:19)? Scripture tells us what we need to know about ourselves and only what we are able to know. What we are able to know about ourselves piques our interest about what we are unable to know. What we are unable to know should warn us against confident systematic accounts of the human personality.

For Scripture presents man as a unity rather than as a sum of distinct parts. It emphasizes what about him is essential, vital, permanent, and substantial over against what is inessential, trivial, temporal, and deceptively apparent. It contrasts what man can know about himself with what only God can know about him. It offers no tidy taxonomy of his created powers.

8

THE IMAGE OF GOD

Our models of the human personality can never rise to a full account of the natural powers put into us by our Creator. The inadequacy of such models is compounded by the daunting truth of man's being made in his Creator's image (Gen. 1:26–27). Only God knows all He did when He "breathed into [man's] nostrils the breath of life; and man became a living soul" (Gen. 2:7), or that He yet does when He "lighteth every man that cometh into the world" (John 1:9). We can only speculate about the nature and extent of the divine image implanted in us and about its full implications. For the self divulged in Scripture is ultimately a mystery. It must remain a mystery because of the mysterious nature of its Creator, Who put into it something of Himself—something indefinable, inaccessible, impenetrably subtle and complex. He shadowed Himself uniquely and mysteriously in His creature man.

To say that man has something of the divine in him is not at all to say that man is in any way personally divine. Unregenerate fallen man opposes God, bearing in only partial, blurred form the implanted image of his Creator and remaining deeply alienated from

Him. Regenerated man is God's redeemed child, within whom the Spirit of God contends with the powers of his fallen nature, restoring the divine image lost in the fall. He is not to any degree himself God. And yet in a manner and to an extent he will never understand, he is indwelt by God (John 14:17, 23).

In fact, believers in Christ are said to be "partakers of the divine nature" (2 Peter 1:4). Paul, with an amazing expression, prays that the Ephesians "might be filled with all the fulness of God" (Eph. 3:19). It is this mysterious participation of the self, most notably of the redeemed self, in the nature of God that will always and finally defeat analysis of its structure and its parts. God drops a veil over the recesses of our own nature as He does over His own.

This mystery pertains to our spiritual responses. Clearly there is something more deeply rooted in us than reason or emotion that sets our attitudes toward God. Scripture leaves undisclosed the source of the human impulse toward the Creator and the manner of its divine prompting. Theologians have divided over the mystery of the human part in salvation: whether divine grace simply enables or actually determines the sinner's choice of God. The inspired psalmist tells us only, "He fashioneth their hearts alike; he considereth all their works" (33:15). It is wise to leave the matter there.

It follows from chapter 5 that when combating the remnants of Freudian thought or the materialist concepts of mental health we must not form our thinking simply in counter relation to theirs, making their positives our negatives and their negatives our positives. Our concept of the self must rise naturally from its own base on what is given us in Scripture, not from the position we seek to demolish. To combat the error of Freudianism, we need not deny the existence of the unconscious while yet insisting that the conscious should rule the unconscious. To defend against the materialists, we need not deny the subtle interweaving of our mental and physical selves. Scripture itself tells us, "A sound heart is the life of the flesh" (Prov. 14:30). The reverse is true also. Whereas "a merry heart doeth good ["causeth good healing," RV, marg.] like a medicine . . . a broken spirit drieth the bones" (17:22). To correct against New Age intuitionism, we need not banish feeling from serious thought, for right thinking and right feeling intertwine in all that is vital about us and our relationship with God. Wisdom begins in "the fear of the Lord" (Ps. 111:10).

In particular we must not fall into the error of the simplified self. Secularists simplify the personality and complicate life into a moral puzzle. They do so in order to dispense with moral responsibility. God does the opposite. He leaves the self mysterious and presents life as a matter of simple choices. He sets the God-blessed life plainly before us, within reach of us all.

THE DESIRING SELF

And if a Levite come from any of thy gates out of all Israel, where he sojourned . . . with all the desire of his mind unto the place which the Lord shall choose; then he shall minister in the name of the Lord his God.

Deuteronomy 18:6–7

9

THE DIGNITY AND WORTH
OF THE FEELINGS

In reacting against what modern psychology has to say about the emotional life, we must not return to the reigning model of the self before Freud and the materialists. Plato's God was transcendent intellect. The God, or divine principle, of the pantheistic Stoics was universal all-determining reason. Later Platonists revised somewhat the concept of their master into a deity of love; but it was an intellectual love, self-absorbed, severely aloof, unconsciously overflowing in acts of creation. The God of these philosophical traditions was an intellectualized final cause or dynamic principle, coldly unaware of its imperfect creation. It diminished the feelings in our inherited view of the self.

Platonism influenced the early church fathers, encouraging a conception of God that emphasized world transcendence and reason. So also did Stoicism, whose dogmas included the suppression of personal desire and acquiescence in one's providentially predetermined destiny. Thus it was that when the Protestant reformers found in Augustine support for their evangelical doctrine, they also found a presiding sense of the overwhelming otherness of God that diminishes man to mere nothingness and dissolves man's purposes in an all-determining will of God. They, like Augustine, would relate passionately to their God, but His majestic transcendence and inscrutable, absolute will shaped their spiritual experience. In contrast with the humanized theology of the Catholic Church, with its provision for human merit in salvation, this consciousness elevated God and restored the biblical doctrines of salvation. It laid the groundwork for Protestant belief, while giving Puritan theology a certain severity of tone.

We indeed owe much to our great evangelical predecessors. We must recognize the loftiness of our God in order to appreciate well His descent to the small matters of His creation. Also, in these times of casual familiarity in sacred matters, the Reformation emphasis on the transcendent majesty and perfect holiness of God—that which raises Him above His creatures—is sorely needed. But there is also to be recognized what the Lord kept impressing upon His disciples and constantly demonstrated in His dealings with them. I refer to the affectionate friendliness of the Savior—His sympathetic interaction with the least of their personal concerns, His attention to their desires and disappointments, to their hopes and fears. He called them His friends (John 15:14–15).

For an austere, distant, unfeeling Being is Plato's God, not ours. A distant impersonal universal rational principle determining all that is and occurs belongs to the Stoics, not to the Scriptures. How different is the minutely attentive, passionately desiring God we see in the person of the Savior. His sensitive encounters with the Samaritan woman at the well, with Nicodemus at night, with the distraught sisters at Bethany, with a guilt-stricken, dejected Peter at the lake, betoken a kindly, affectionate regard for individual humanity, not just for man in the abstract or in the mass. Let it never be thought that the Son of God died for just a species or part of a species. He "loved Martha, and her sister, and Lazarus" (John 11:5). He surnamed at least three of His disciples (Mark 3:17–18). He took note of many that appear with names in Scripture because of His notice and of many others, such as the poor widow with her mite, who do not. The Master knew not only the stars by name.

It will not do to say that the emotional behavior of our Savior is an anthropomorphism—a merely humanized expression of His true self—and therefore a feature of His manner that can be filtered out of what He came to reveal to us of God. When He assured the disciples that "he that hath seen me hath seen the Father" (John 14:9) on the night before His crucifixion, He was speaking of His love for them and affectionately attending to their fears. When He declared Himself Lord of the temple and rid it of the merchandisers, His anger was one with His action. The weeping mourners at Lazarus's tomb found an answerable grief in the Savior. A distraught father must never have forgotten the tender expression with which He addressed the body of his twelve-year-old daughter: "Talitha [Little Lamb] . . . I say unto thee, arise" (Mark 5:41). Perhaps the most striking sense of God we have from the example of Christ is that He is a fervently desiring Being and that associated with His desiring are emotions we find in ourselves.

Expressions of divine feeling are not limited to the Gospels. Echoing throughout the writings of the Old Testament prophets is the passionate plea of a desiring God. In Jehovah's words to Judah through Jeremiah we hear what G. Campbell Morgan called "the challenge of wounded love."[1] "What iniquity have your fathers found in me, that they are gone far from me, and have walked after vanity, and are become vain?" "Have I been a wilderness unto Israel? a land of darkness?" "Can a maid forget her ornaments, or a bride her attire? yet my people have forgotten me days without number." "Turn, O backsliding children, saith the Lord; for I am married to you" (Jer. 2:5, 31–32; 3:14). Through Jeremiah's contemporary in Babylon, Ezekiel, comes a cry of divine anguish: "I am broken with their whorish heart" (Ezek. 6:9).

Wounded love can turn to fury. "Thou hast forsaken me, saith the Lord, thou art gone backward: therefore will I stretch out my hand against thee, and destroy thee; I am weary with repenting" (Jer. 15:6). The language is of fervent love stretched past the breaking point yet still solicitous of the one beloved. The fury graciously can be assuaged. Of repentant Israel God says, "I will love them freely; for mine anger is turned away from him" (Hosea 14:4). Of redeemed Israel He says, "As the bridegroom rejoiceth over the bride, so shall thy God rejoice over thee" (Isa. 62:5). Again, "The Lord thy God . . . will rejoice over thee with joy; he will rest in his love, he will joy over thee with singing" (Zeph. 3:17). The Jehovah of the Old Testament like the Jesus of the New is passionately involved with His people.

The same sensitivity and fervor so evident in the Savior appear in persons who have matured in godliness. We meet them in Scripture as in common life. We rightly think of Paul as a brilliant logician, master disputer, in command of vast intellectual resources both rabbinical and Hellenic. We may forget what overshadows even his powers of reasoning: Paul's deeply affectionate nature, his tender, sympathizing spirit. Hear him as he greets his friends in a congregation he has never visited—twenty-five of them by name. Among them are one Rufus "and his mother and mine," a woman who evidently had taken charge of Paul's needs, as mothers do, in both word and deed (Rom. 16:13).

Having finished his instructions to his converts at Philippi—his "brethren," he calls them—Paul urges them in the most passionate terms not to waver from what he has taught them. "Therefore, my brethren dearly beloved and longed for, my joy and crown, so stand fast in the Lord, my dearly beloved" (Phil. 4:1). Writing from Rome on behalf of a converted runaway slave he is returning to his Christian master, Paul requests a merciful response that will "refresh my bowels in the Lord" (Philem. 20). Can anyone doubt the friendliness of Paul and, entwined with that, the huge part that richly developed feelings played in his life and ministry? The transformed Paul, fierce persecutor of believers in Christ, appears most remarkable in his emotional nature.

Paul knew negative feelings as well. His spirits could flag. It was evidently with some anxiety that Paul the prisoner, having escaped shipwreck, trudged under guard toward Rome. Some miles from the great city on the Appian Way he was heartened by a delegation of Roman believers, "whom when Paul saw, he thanked God, and took courage" (Acts 28:15). To the Corinthians Paul acknowledges, "I was with you in weakness, and in fear, and in much trembling" (1 Cor. 2:3). Writing later, he shows a capacity to be emotionally wounded, for they had hurt him. "I will very gladly spend and be spent for you; though the more abundantly I love you, the less I be loved" (2 Cor. 12:15). How poignant are these echoes in Paul of Jeremiah's grieving God.

One can hardly fail to notice the part that feelings play in the fruit of the Spirit described by Paul in Galatians 5. Among the attributes of spiritual maturity listed here are love, joy, long-suffering, peace, gentleness—all expressions of the emotional life. Peter's ladder of spiritual growth in his second Epistle rises to "brotherly kindness" and "charity" (1:5–7). The feelings exist not merely to be subjugated and denied but rather to be activated and ordered in the good will and purpose of God.

Is it any wonder that God speaks to man and man to God in poetry so often in Scripture?—about 40 percent of the time in the Old Testament according to one rough estimate. It is poetry not cold prose that best carries the truths of human duty to the dim regions of the heart where attitudes are set and life stances are formed. Jacob chose poetry for his final words to his sons (Gen. 49). God had Moses write a poem and teach it to Israel to embody His final challenge to the people, one to be remembered and heeded. His words "shall drop as the rain" and "distil as the dew"—that is, will penetrate with gentle irresistible power (Deut. 32:2). It is the poetry of the Hebrew Scriptures that is cited most often by New Testament writers to drive home important truths.

For man is not adequately conceived in Greek fashion as a reasoning animal or in Roman fashion as coldly locked into his destiny by universal reason and will. He is a being that loves—in ways that no other animal can. His deepest desire is to be loved and valued worthily—a desire able to be fulfilled when he freely responds to the same desire in his Creator and Redeemer. It is not just his reasoning apparatus that dignifies him and makes him desired by God and able to return the love of God. It is also, and especially, the feeling, desiring part—that which in the smallest child can respond to God and be offered to God as a gift. This above all He would have and shape into a reflection of Himself. He would form in us, as in David, a man after His own heart.

10

THE DIGNITY AND DUTY OF DESIRE

Because God fervently desires, we do also. Because He loves, and yearns for what He loves in His fallen creature, we love also and yearn for what we love. Desire is created into us. Socrates spoke a truth when he said that the one thing fundamental about every person is that he desires for himself good and not evil.

The problem for us, said Socrates, is to get clear what the good truly is and what it is not. That problem is addressed throughout Scripture. It is characteristic of flawed humanity not to know its own good. God knows our true good and has revealed it to us. It is what He desires for us. The master theme of Deuteronomy is that Israel, in choosing for God, would also be choosing its own true good. God's good and Israel's were one and the same. Israel's truest self-interest was intertwined with God's.

God puts His commands behind our good so He can bring us to it. He commands us to follow the path of our benefit. Pharaoh spoke in this manner to Joseph when he commanded the good of Joseph's family. "Say unto thy brethren, This do ye; lade your beasts, and go, get you unto the land of Canaan; and take your father and your households, and come unto me: and I will give you the good of the land of Egypt, and ye shall eat the fat of the land. Now thou art commanded, this do ye" (Gen. 45:17–19). Jesus commanded the weary "and heavy laden" to come to Him and accept His yoke so He could give them "rest" (Matt. 11:28–29). God works by command and entreaty and, when these fail, by blunt circumstance to raise our desires to coincide with our own good—to have us seek what will benefit and not harm us.

Personal desire is not in itself an enemy to our good, to what God desires for us. Both the Epicureans and the Stoics taught the shrinking of desire to a point where disappointment is impossible. The goal was to arrive at a passive tranquility of mind rendering one impervious to ill fortune. Christian pietism has at times done the same by urging a severe spirituality devoid of personal desire and earthly interests. This is not biblical spirituality, which on the contrary makes grateful use of all blessings, immaterial and material, generously provided by the One "who giveth us richly all things to enjoy" (1 Tim. 6:17).

How easy it is, in rejecting pride and covetousness, to condemn all self-concern as sinful, assuming that it flows from a corrupt, rebellious center. Scripture constantly appeals to its readers and hearers to act in their best interests, to show wise self-concern, to have an accurate sense of their own good and act upon it. Physical desire is directed toward the satisfaction of physical needs and the perpetuation of the species. Spiritual desire is directed toward the satisfaction of spiritual needs and toward the proliferation of spiritual progeny—those who will respond to the invitation of the new birth.

God is equally the author of each. He associates pleasure with important physical and spiritual desires and enjoys gratifying both desires well beyond mere necessity. These desires can connect with false as well as true values, and there must always be a respect for authenticity and scale. Nevertheless, God put objective value in everything He created; and we may, and indeed must, order our desires in accordance with His delights, delights that extend even to the perishable flowers of the field. It is right to care about what He cares about and enjoys. All the trees of the garden, not only the forbidden one, were "pleasant to the sight, and good for food" (Gen. 2:9).

John Calvin himself speaks to this point when he warns against "that inhuman philosophy which, in allowing no use of the creatures but for necessity, not only maliciously deprives us of the lawful fruit of the divine beneficence, but cannot be realized without depriving man of all his senses, and reducing him to a block." The passage is worth citing at length. God created food "not only for our necessity, but also for our delight." He provided "in herbs, fruits, and trees, besides their various uses, gracefulness of appearance and sweetness of smell." Calvin asks, "Has the Lord adorned flowers with all the beauty which spontaneously presents itself to the eye, and the sweet odour which delights the sense of smell, and shall it be unlawful for us to enjoy that beauty and this odour? What? Has he not so distinguished colours as to make some more agreeable than others? Has he not given qualities to gold and silver, ivory and marble, thereby rendering them precious above other metals or stones? In short, has he not given many things a value without having any necessary use?"[1] Scripture sanctifies our desires for what God has created to please us, for these desires align with His.

We human beings are the chief objects of God's desire in His earthly creation. We have been created "a little lower than the angels" (Ps. 8:5) and in the resurrection will be "equal unto the angels" (Luke 20:36). Our Lord cares about even the most trivial matters of our earthly existence that may trouble us: "even the very hairs of your head are all numbered" (Luke 12:7). Jesus knew how to buoy the flagging spirits of His disciples with comforting words of their importance to Him: "Fear not, little flock; for it is your Father's good pleasure to give you the kingdom" (Luke 12:32). When the Lord's sheep stumble or stray,

He does not deal with the lost or broken objects of His love as Satan does with his objects of temporary interest. The Good Shepherd is at pains to rescue and restore the wandering sheep (Luke 15). Jesus desired that His disciples not be deceived about the value to Him of the objects of His care.

When we realize that God cares about us even more than we can possibly care about ourselves, we can more easily receive what He would drive deep into our thoughts: that our truest desires, toward what is best for us, and His own toward us are in perfect agreement. Satan makes it his business to persuade us that our good is at odds with God's. Satan is of course the great fabricator of false goods, which he constantly merchandizes as genuine. He encourages deceitful desires and supplies them with false ware. Just as when he tempted the Lord in the wilderness, He proposes to us a competitive model of values that places God's good in conflict with ours. He would keep us from recognizing that it is in our best interest to act in God's interest, just as it is in God's interest that we act in our own best interest. When we come to understand that our good and God's agree, God has us exactly where He wants us—where we can flourish in His will. To understand this fundamental truth and let it possess us is to have taken a giant stride toward Christian maturity.

Still, a proposition so strange as this—that self-concern is both allowable and necessary—will require substantial support from Scripture. One does not have to look far. The appeal to self-interest is everywhere in the sacred writings. Time and again Israel was urged to obey Jehovah "for thy good" (Deut. 10:13). Immediately upon Israel's consent to obey the commandments brought by Moses came the anguished reply of Jehovah to a people who knew not their own good. "O that there were such an heart in them, that they would fear me, and keep all my commandments always, that it might be well with them, and with their children for ever" (Deut. 5:29). God's commands were grounded in His desire for His people's good, and it was urgent that they understand that. "Keep therefore the words of this covenant, and do them, that ye may prosper in all that ye do" (Deut. 29:9).

The Psalms make clear that to move toward God is to move toward one's good, a happy condition of life, and that to forsake God is to forsake good. "Surely goodness and mercy will follow" the godly man of Psalm 1, in sad contrast to the life path of the ungodly man, whose way "shall perish." Self-interest comes into play repeatedly in Proverbs: "If thou be wise, thou shalt be wise for thyself: but if thou scornest, thou alone shalt bear it" (9:12). Again, "He that getteth wisdom loveth his own soul: he that keepeth understanding shall find good" (19:8).

Throughout the Prophetic Books sounds the twofold divine appeal to apostate Israel: Is it right what you are doing to Me? Is it good what you are doing to yourselves? "Seek good, and not evil, that ye may live," preaches Amos (5:14). "Sow *to yourselves* in righteousness" (10:12; italics mine) is the cry of God through Hosea. Personal cost assessment is urged in Jehovah's words to His people through Isaiah: "I am the Lord thy God which teacheth thee to profit. . . . O that thou hadst hearkened to my commandments! then had thy peace been as a river, and thy righteousness as the waves of the sea" (48:17–18). Similarly through Jeremiah, He says, "Hath a nation changed their gods, which are yet no gods? but my people have changed their glory for that which doth not profit" (2:11).

In Jeremiah's opening message, the horror of Israel's revolt from God is said to be twofold: "My people have committed two evils; they have forsaken me the fountain of living waters, and hewed them out cisterns . . . that can hold no water" (2:13). The "two evils" are the wrong toward God and the harm to themselves. The latter evil is especially noted in Jeremiah's prophecy. Israel, in forgetting God, has neglected her own glory: "Can a maid forget her ornaments, or a bride her attire? yet my people have forgotten me days without number" (2:32). Israel's sins "have withholden good things from you" (5:25). "Hast thou not procured this unto thyself?" (2:17). The people must understand that in sinning against God they have acted "against themselves" (11:17).

There will be a time, promises God, when His people will no longer offend Him and harm themselves, when their desires and His will be fully realized. "I will give them one heart, and one way, that they may fear me for ever, for the good of them, and of their children after them. . . . I will rejoice over them, to do them good" (Jer. 32:39, 41). Here and elsewhere in the Old Testament, the issue of spiritual obligation is pressed relentlessly in terms of a double duty—to God and to oneself.

The New Testament, like the Old, continually reminds its readers and hearers of their true good. "We know that all things work together for good to them that love God, to them who are the called according to his purpose," declares Paul in a well-known passage (Rom. 8:28). Heavenly good beckons those who follow the Savior. So also does earthly good. "He that will love life, and see good days . . . let him eschew evil, and do good," writes Peter (1 Pet. 3:10–11). These and other passages imply that an accurate sense of self-interest can encourage godly living.

It can also motivate sacrificial commitment. Peter spoke for the disciples when he raised the question of payback. "Behold, we have forsaken all, and followed thee; what shall we have therefore?" (Matt. 19:27). Jesus surprisingly did not chide Peter for wrong thinking. He did not tell him "Thoughts of self have no place in My kingdom." He did not respond as we would to such a question: "Now Peter, you should not be thinking that way." Jesus answered, in effect, "A lot!" and did so with emphasis. "Verily I say unto you, There is no man that hath left house, or brethren, or sisters, or father, or mother, or wife, or children, or lands, for my sake, and the gospel's, but he shall receive an hundredfold now in this time, houses, and brethren, and sisters, and mothers, and children, and lands, with persecutions; and in the world to come eternal life" (Mark 10:29–30). The Lord never asked His disciples to abandon their own good for His. He asked them to relinquish lesser goods for a greater one.

In an equally remarkable passage, which were it not Scripture might seem demeaning in putting the divine Paymaster under obligation to His servants, believers are assured that "God is not unrighteous to forget your work and labour of love, which ye have shewed toward his name" (Heb. 6:10). We can trust God to do what is right toward us in recompensing our labors. Even a cup of cold water given in His name will have its reward (Matt. 10:42). Paul may have remembered these words of the Lord when he wrote, "Whatsoever good thing any man doeth, the same shall he receive of the Lord" (Eph. 6:8).

Indeed, an expectation of reward is part of faith as defined in Hebrews, where it is coupled with belief in God's existence: "He that cometh to God must believe that he is, and that he is a rewarder of them that diligently seek him" (11:6). "He that reapeth receiveth wages," said the Lord Himself (John 4:36), Who will have reward on His mind when He returns (Rev. 22:12).

Neither Paul nor John, who surely followed Christ from higher motives, thought it beneath him to regard his eternal reward (1 Cor. 9:17–18; 2 John 8). Neither considered an interest in reward incompatible with the paramount constraint of their service, "the love of Christ" (2 Cor. 5:14), and it was not theologically embarrassing to them to express it. Peter reminded suffering believers that they had been "thereunto called" that they might "inherit a blessing" (1 Pet. 3:9). This blessing is "an inheritance incorruptible . . . reserved in heaven for you" (1 Pet. 1:4). Peter no doubt was remembering the words of the Lord in the Sermon on the Mount, where He commanded His disciples to "lay up *for yourselves*" durable treasures in heaven (Matt. 6:20; italics mine). Paul likewise may have had in mind his Lord's encouragement for the persecuted—"for great is your reward in heaven"—when he comforted his fellow sufferers with the assurance that "our light affliction, which is but for a moment, worketh for us a far more exceeding and eternal weight of glory" (Matt. 5:12; 2 Cor. 4:17). True discipleship is something owed to the Master, and that motive must emphatically remain primary. But it is also a prudential matter—a duty, we may say, to ourselves.

What the apostles exemplify for us here is in no way a shrewd cost-benefit calculation based on promised reciprocity. They followed the Lord, in G. Campbell Morgan's phrase, "independently of advantage"[2]—that is, with a loyalty not rooted in considerations of personal gain. But in the Christian life, just as in a good marriage, there occurs a coinciding of desires and interests so that something done for the other is also done for oneself. When one benefits, the other sees himself or herself as also benefiting. Something done in loving sacrifice by the one will be met by a comparable response of the other so as not to leave an arrears of generosity on either side. Both will take it upon themselves not to be outdone in recompense, in over-going recompense, for reasons not of equity but of love.

There is a time for a parent to say to a son or daughter, "You owe me obedience because of who I am." This consideration is surely primary. There is also a time for a parent to say, "I can do a great deal for a child who will obey me. If you serve me in the way I ask, I can then serve you in the way you need and in the way, if you only knew it, you truly desire."

For Christians then, God's good must be the primary motive in discipleship, self-good a collateral motive, though not for that reason a negligible one. The true disciple seeks *first* the kingdom of God" (Matt. 6:33; italics mine). He does not seek first to please himself and expect his pleasing of God to come as value added. And yet for the sinner coming to Christ for salvation, the reverse is likely the case. The eternal danger of his soul and the present poverty of his life are foremost in his mind, with his desire to please God an associated but collateral motive. He comes indeed because "God so loved." But he comes also and especially that he "should not perish, but have everlasting life" (John 3:16).

This two-sided truth is striking in Paul, who while pronouncing covetousness to be "idolatry" (Col. 3:5) urged the Corinthians to "covet earnestly the best gifts" (1 Cor. 12:31). They should covet especially "to prophesy," to speak understandably to a congregation, rather than to babble unintelligibly in an unknown tongue (1 Cor. 14:39). But beyond the gifts of ministry that Paul lists was what was most to be sought: charity, the crown of the virtues (1 Cor. 13:1). The recipients of the Epistle were to covet in the right direction. Their desire to gain and possess would then aim toward others' good as well as toward their own.

The Christian slaves in Ephesus were to serve their masters "as the servants of Christ, doing the will of God from the heart . . . knowing that whatsoever good thing any man doeth, the same shall he receive of the Lord, whether he be bond or free" (Eph. 6:6–8). Their obedience would be compensated if not by their masters then by God. It was a motivating principle Paul thought worth mentioning. It would unite their own good with the good of another, their master, and most importantly with the good of God.

11

THE RANKING OF LOVES

How do we distinguish the proper and necessary concern for personal good from the egoistic self-love condemned by God in which covetous purposes—what Scripture calls the imaginations of the heart—flow forth and return in an endless loop of vain desire and frustration? We find our answer as always in Scripture, which instructs us in the right ordering of our loves.

We are admonished in 1 John to "love not the world, neither the things that are in the world" (2:15). John gives two reasons for not doing so. One is prudential: "the world passeth away, and the lust thereof" (1 John 2:17). It is foolish to center desire on something that will not last. "Wilt thou set thine eyes upon that which is not?" asks the proverb (Prov. 23:5). "The workman made it: therefore it is not God," declares Hosea with fine scorn (8:6). Not only the objects of such desires are insubstantial; the desire for them—"the lust thereof"—will disappear. Phantom values are a foolish choice and a dangerous trap. It is wise to beware. Here as elsewhere God commands us to pursue our true good. Biblical self-concern distinguishes between true and false values.

The other reason given by John gives an even more compelling basis for distinguishing right from wrong self-concern. "If any man love the world, the love of the Father is not in him" (1 John 2:15). This reason speaks of a contrast in loves. A self-concern driven by "the lust of the flesh, and the lust of the eyes, and the pride of life" dethrones God in the mind, displacing what must be the chief desire, the love of God.

From blind, misplaced desire stems the condition of mind Satan accomplished in Eve and Adam and attempted in his attack on the Son of God in the wilderness. In this mind state love for God and self-love are placed in competition so that one negates the other. Jesus warned the disciples that the love of God excludes all other mastering loves. "No man can serve two masters," He said. "Ye cannot serve God and mammon" (Matt. 6:24). The love of God has an absolute claim on the soul, which if subordinated to lesser loves is in effect rejected.

Satan's model of loves and duties displaces the highest love and in so doing disorders them all, setting them at odds. Satan knows that to degrade a love from its proper position is to destroy its force, for its power depends upon a recognition of its status. Given time and means, the dislocation of a higher love can prove disastrous for the entire ranking. If it is the highest love, of God, that is supplanted, the result, whether for an individual or a society, will be moral anarchy and spiritual ruin. When financial goals are allowed to displace the love of God in a life, then care for family and for personal health and appearance as well as for the finer things of life can tumble with it, not to speak of the damage to character and reputation. When right subordination is observed and the highest love kept in place, the downward levels become mutually enforcing and enhancing, value is distributed and scaled truly, and all objects of value are respected in a manner and to a degree approved by God. When God is put first, all other things take their proper place.

This truth was laid out by Augustine, who saw all virtues as loves. These loves embrace the entire work of the Creator. There is, he said, a degree of virtuous love suitable to the smallest and seemingly least significant object of creation for the very reason that God made it and it must therefore have interested Him. God cares for and enjoys His flowers and birds. He seems indeed to enjoy His lions and vultures, His river-horse splashing amongst the reeds, His leviathan thrashing in the sea—creatures fearsome or repulsive to Job (Job 38–39). God cares about creatures beneath our notice as we care about our pets and other domestic animals. He observes their gestation and sees when they give birth (Job 39:1–3). He is there when they "fall on the ground" to die (Matt. 10:29).

Here Scripture may seem to be in conflict with itself. We are told not to love the world but also told that God Himself does so and He is our example. God, we well know, "loved the world" enough to sacrifice His Son to restore it and still loves it in His ongoing work of redemption. This work includes not only mankind but also the rest of His creation. Despite sin's disturbance of His creative work, God still values what He originally produced and participates sympathetically in the "groans," as it were in the birth pains, of its restoration (Rom. 8:19–26). To love the world is not to love God, but to love God is to love what He loves, and His loves include the world of His creation. What is the solution to this paradox?

Though the Son of God, like His Father, loved the world of His making, He did not love the world offered to Him by Satan in the temptation, the world systems Satan controls by means of the lust of the eyes, the lust of the flesh, and the pride of life. This worldly love is sinful and vain. Yet we may love God's creative work after His example, and indeed ought to so long as we love it in the way He does. We love it less than we love Him. We love persons more than things, as He does. But our love for Him embraces all the objects of His handiwork and implies a degree of obligation toward all objects created for our pleasure and granted us for our care.

It is true, and deserves emphasis, that even the good things of creation, those God Himself cares for and cares about, can become sinful preoccupations if our love for them is allowed to outrank our love for God. Music is a worthy love but not if it is loved more than God. Children ought to be loved as God loves them, but even parental love can be idolatrous if it exceeds a love for God. And so it is with all our worthy attachments. "Lovest thou me more than these?" was the searching question put to Peter by the Savior (John 21:15). It is evil to worship and serve the creation more than the Creator (Rom. 1:25), even in things legitimate and benign. Yet Scripture sanctions an affection for the natural goods that come to us from above, fleeting as they may be, if we receive them gratefully and in a wisely discriminating way.

Duties derive from loves and are coranked with them. This truth was available to Israel long before it was restated by Jesus. When challenged by a Pharisee to enunciate the first commandment in the Law—the highest of all duties—Jesus quoted Deuteronomy 6:4–5. "Hear, O Israel: The Lord our God is one Lord: and thou shalt love the Lord thy God with all thine heart, and with all thy soul, and with all thy might." He coupled the first commandment with a second commandment "like unto" the first, quoting from Leviticus 19:18: "Thou shalt love thy neighbour as thyself." Having conjoined these duties from the Hebrew Scriptures, Jesus underscored their fundamental, all-inclusive importance. "On these two commandments hang all the law and the prophets" (Matt. 22:37–40). That matters of duty are matters of love was reiterated by Paul, when he wrote that "love is the fulfilling of the law" (Rom. 13:10).

A proper ordering of loves justifies and even enforces love in proper scale for all objects to which God has assigned value. The love of God requires the love of one's neighbor, and the love of one's neighbor requires as a benchmark the love of one's self. The love of one's body is a benchmark for the love of one's wife (Eph. 5:28–29). The implications are vast. Until a man loves God supremely, he cannot love his wife and children as he should. He cannot care about his acquaintances and other fellow human beings as fully and truly as he should. He cannot rightly love even himself.

This two-sided truth—that the exclusive love for God ("with all thine heart") is not exclusive—lies at the heart of our understanding the love of ourselves. Satan would have us think we must love either God or ourselves, persuading some to choose love of self over God, and others from sincere love of God to reject natural personal desires from a false sense of spiritual duty. Heaven smiles on passionate human love in the Song of Songs. There is warmth in the description of Jacob's long service for Rachel—seven years which "seemed unto him but a few days, for the love he had to her" (Gen. 29:20). One of earth's wonders for Solomon was "the way of a man with a maid" (Prov. 30:19).

Satan also tries to convince us that love of others must compete with love of self, when the deep truth is that putting others' good ahead of one's own in no way threatens one's own good. We have noted that when a husband in sacrificial, affectionate love seeks his wife's good, he is also, without intending so, gaining his own. His love will be returned with interest. A surpassing concern for the good of others and beyond that for the good of God is the condition for one's own good and the means of enlarging it. It is an inescapable universal truth that all good flows from subordination within the will of God.

This subordination distributes value without diminishing it. Explaining subordination in the family structure, Paul finds an example in the executive order of the Godhead, in which the Son accepts the headship of the Father not just from duty but voluntarily from mutual love. So should the husband be subject to Christ, his Head, and the wife to her head, the husband—an order elaborated in Ephesians 5. In fact, all should "be subject one to another, and be clothed with humility," wrote Peter (1 Pet. 5:5). Peter was quick to add that the way of submission is not the way of personal loss. "Humble yourselves therefore under the mighty hand of God, that he may exalt you in due time" (1 Pet. 5:6; see also Luke 14:11; 18:14). "All things are yours," said Paul, whether "things present, or things to come; all are yours; and ye are Christ's; and Christ is God's" (1 Cor. 3:21–23).

Even small enjoyments may be considered "ours." The prophet speaks of happier times to come in Israel when "the streets of the city shall be full of boys and girls playing in the streets thereof" (Zech. 8:5). May we not suppose that just as God values the delights of children, He is pleased to grant us our delights as we keep our loves in their proper order? The delicate touches of His artistry in a beautiful sunset need not be beneath our notice. Nor need we ignore the beauty of a flower or in the song of a bird. The works of gifted musicians and painters and craftsman in joyous imitation of His own creative skill have their rightful place in our estimation. If He cares enough about what we might consider trifles of His creation to shower attention upon them, beautifying them beyond necessity, dressing them in fragile splendor, He must care about the small objects of our interests and desires as well.

When we put the love of God foremost, we embrace an entire universe of values in which each love is rightly directed and enhanced. All that is false and perverse in self-love—the lusts of eyes and flesh, the pride of life; competitive self-serving and self-honoring—is excluded. All loves are rectified and adjusted to one another in due downward honor—harmonized, enriched, and enhanced. We may love ourselves truly when, and only when, we truly and more greatly love our God.

12

DESIRE'S DELIGHTS
AND SORROWS

The first fact then about a committed Christian is the priority of his love for God. He finds that this love, preferred above all others, distributes his other loves in proper order and presides over them in a fulfilling way.

Among his other loves is a measured regard for his own good. It is a two-sided truth that in desiring chiefly the good of God and secondarily the good of others he loses nothing of his own good but rather enlarges it. Christian love "seeketh not her own" (1 Cor. 13:5), yet God sees to it that nothing sought for His or others' good goes unrequited. Everything we give to God or to others in His name He returns to us with interest. Though this return is not the reason we do our giving, it is no less true for not being the reason for our doing so. God intends our sense of self-good to be bonded to His good and to others' good.

The love of God ranks other loves according to the values of their objects. We may speak of these loves as desires, and their objects as things to be possessed or accomplished. The range of our loves can be as great as God's. We can look with interest and affection on all the objects God has created. We may desire them for ourselves to a degree appropriate to their value and within the limits of rightful possession. The uppermost desire for God will in no way lessen the desire of a bride or a bridegroom to possess the other, but it may well level down the desire to possess a fine automobile or an expensive watch.

We can desire to see something important and far reaching accomplished for God ("Thy kingdom come") or for others ("that [Israel] might be saved," Rom. 10:1) or for ourselves ("that I may know him, and the power of his resurrection, and the fellowship of his sufferings, being made conformable unto his death," Phil. 3:10). Though we would not mention it in the same breath, we may also legitimately nurture a desire for a house to buy rather than rent, for a pair of attractive and comfortable shoes, for a birthday party to be carried off with success, for some recently planted shrubs to flourish, or for a school team to do its best in a tournament. All are acceptable subjects for prayer. In God's register of values, a lesser good need not be disdained because a greater is greater, or a greater because it is not the greatest of all.

Consider the range of objects mentioned in Scripture. We read of animals and birds, of plants and precious stones, of seasons and weather, of mountains and streams and bodies of water, of crops and insects, of everyday things such as pots and ovens, cooking oil and seasonings—all in splendid profusion and variety. Objects worthy of God's benign attention are also worthy of our interest and desire. Israel was to "go up and possess" the land reserved for them by God and to enjoy it (Deut. 1:21). Israelites were to go about their lives honoring God and appreciating His bounty. They could appreciate the delicacy of roasted quail, but not to the extent of complaining about their daily manna in the wilderness, raising their love of food above their love of God (Exod. 16:13; Num. 11:31–33). Job showed a godly ranking of values when he declared, "I have esteemed the words of his mouth more than my necessary food" (23:12). Yet Scripture does not censure a love of good food and drink. The wine Jesus created from water was of the very best (John 2:10). Evidently we may care about lesser goods so long as we care about them in the way and to the degree that God does and do not covet what is another's.

God also recognizes what we know as sentimental or symbolic value. He knows that the small things we treasure may have a value for us far beyond their ordinary worth, and He respects that value. The prophet Nathan's account of a poor man's "little ewe lamb" that "grew up together with him, and with his children," and "did eat of his own meat, and drank of his own cup, and lay in his bosom, and was unto him as a daughter" shows a sympathetic regard for personal value. The lamb was a special possession to its owner, an object of tender, affectionate care, but to the rich man, and from a practical viewpoint, was only something to serve to one's guests (2 Sam. 12:3). The coin lost and recovered by the woman in Jesus' parable in Luke 15 may very well, if some commentators are right, have had more personal than inherent value. She was driven to find it with a zeal in excess of what another might think suitable to its worth. The gain and loss of what we affectionately possess can move us to a degree beyond its ordinary value. A letter or photo might be the first object we would save from a fire.

God would have us voice our desires to Him in our prayers, and He promises to respond (Matt. 7:7–11). The conditions are that we pray with a heart toward His will and that we persist in praying. It is true that He may not answer our prayers in exactly the way we specify. He will "give good things to them that ask him" (Matt. 7:11) and what we ask for may not be good. For this reason, He presides over our desires not only in a fulfilling way but also in a discriminating way. He sorts and selects and substitutes among them for our own good as well as for His purposes.

Little reflection is needed for us to realize that our desires are very often ill-formed, ill-targeted, or ill-timed, or all of these at once. When we pray, "we know not what we should pray for as we ought" (Rom. 8:26). We often do not know our true needs or even the true desires of our heart. We certainly are limited in knowing the needs of others. Our solution to a problem may not be the best one, and our sense of urgency may not at all be God's and based in reality. But we desire and pray all the same, and God brings our desires and prayers under His discreet management so as to satisfy His purposes and our desires more fully than we could have thought. Unwise yearnings get corrected, unworthy desires fall away, as the Spirit processes our requests, interceding for us "according to the will of God" (Rom. 8:27). In time we may very well be relieved that He has wisely discriminated among our desires. For now, we may very well be burdened with a keen sense of loss.

We should understand that it is entirely natural to feel frustration when desires are unrealized, just as it is natural to feel elation when they are fulfilled. "Hope deferred maketh the heart sick: but when the desire cometh, it is a tree of life" (Prov. 13:12). The course of desire in courtship, as we know, can be tumultuous. "The path of true love never did run smooth," says one of Shakespeare's lovers.[1] Before the enjoyment of hope fulfilled may be the trial of hope under siege by doubts. Before the sadness of hope unfulfilled may have been the transient pleasure of hope euphoric. Desire can be gratified, blocked, redirected, or deferred. Desires themselves can fluctuate. They can disappear as quickly as they appeared. Their order can get shuffled and reshuffled. Especially is this true of the lesser objects of desire. But their flow continues, and their persistency and power to take possession of our thoughts are simple facts of our existence recognized in Scripture. When "desire shall fail," we are ready for the grave (Eccles. 12:5).

It should be a comfort that when the love of God is kept foremost, our chief desire can never be disappointed. We need never lose what matters most to us. God is our faithful provider and friend—an all-wise, all-knowing, all-powerful, ever-gracious, sensitively attentive companion and guide. He keeps His promises with a generous overplus of bounty. He delights in doing more than is asked. His desire for our good far outstrips even our own. Just as a father knows how to give good gifts to his children, the heavenly Father gives us the best gift, the Holy Spirit, to comfort us in distress and to help us defeat what troubles us most, our sin (Luke 11:13). Indeed He gives us Himself, entirely, for all three Persons of the Godhead are said to indwell the believer (John 14:16, 23).

Of the gratification of this highest desire—for God—we can ever be sure. But we can also be sure of the satisfaction of our suitable lesser desires. For "no good thing will he withhold from them that walk uprightly" (Ps. 84:11). When our highest desire is to please God, our worthy lower desires cohere with God's desires for us and therefore are certain of fulfillment in the way most suitable to our needs and deepest yearnings. When our pleasure is to please Him, His pleasure is to please us, for His pleasure and ours align. We are not meant to trudge through life with ever-beckoning unattainable hopes and dreams like those whose lives are purposed toward emptiness, whose rejection of God has doomed them to continual frustration in this world and the next. We have what matters most and what matters best. What God chooses to withhold from us for reasons of His and our good is of little consequence, though we may not feel so at the time.

And that can be much of the time. For we can be far less certain that our lesser desires will be gratified—fulfilled in the manner and time of our wishing—than we can be of our highest desire, whose gratification is always available to us. God knows better than to rubber-stamp all our wishes—one of the most powerful of which is to hold onto what we already have. "The Lord gave, and the Lord hath taken away," said Job, to which he added, "blessed be the name of the Lord" (1:21). We continually lose things that matter to us—some of greater, some of lesser importance. We grieve over what is lost to an extent relative to its felt value and to the finality of the loss. A missing checkbook or billfold, the first dent in a new car, a missed flight, a failed investment, a serious injury to a child, the loss of a job, the loss of a friendship, the grave illness of a spouse, the slur on a reputation—these and numberless other frustrations of desire unsettle us in differing degrees and for differing lengths of time.

As well they might. An imperturbable evenness of spirits is not laid down as a norm in Scripture. Personal gains are occasions for thankful rejoicing. Personal losses are promptings to soul-searching and spiritual attentiveness. They are occasions for God to show His character in bringing something of good from them and in the process mature our character as well. How else might we come to know beauty from ashes, honey in the rock, streams in the desert, a door of hope in the valley of Achor, lives revitalized and refined?

The strength and scope of human desire is sanctified by the example of the Savior. "With desire I have desired to eat this passover with you before I suffer," He said to His disciples before His crucifixion (Luke 22:15). He had spoken before of the eagerness with which He pressed toward the "hour" of His redemptive act. "I have a baptism to be baptized with; and how am I straitened till it be accomplished"

(Luke 12:50). His overmastering desire was to do His Father's will and, while doing it, to succor and strengthen His disciples.

The Lord was subject to lesser desires as well, all of which He kept in due order. He fed a multitude with the contents of a boy's lunch and, we may reasonably suppose, distributed also to Himself and enjoyed it. He also on another occasion, when there was important spiritual work at hand, dismissed His disciples' offer of food with a reminder of priorities: "I have meat to eat that ye know not of. . . . My meat is to do the will of him that sent me, and to finish his work" (John 4:32, 34).

The Lord knew the conflict of desires. In Gethsemane He recoiled from the horror before Him, asking that it might pass from Him, but then acquiesced in the will of the Father, which was also His own: "Not my will, but thine, be done" (Luke 22:42). He proceeded to His sin-bearing death, enduring the cross "for the joy that was set before him" (Heb. 12:2). He surely knew, on a scale we can never know, how desires can pull against each other.

He knew desire deferred also. On the way to Gethsemane, Jesus spoke to the Father in His disciples' hearing about joys yet to come in the final gathering and glorification of His own. "Father, I will that they also, whom thou hast given me, be with me where I am; that they may behold my glory, which thou hast given me" (John 17:24). He would have them with Him where He was going, but it was not to be for a time. Until then His disciples, not without His constant attentive notice and ready assistance, would struggle in a world that rejected Him and that would reject them as well. We sense a divine yearning in the Savior's words for a condition yet to be realized.

We can sense fervent yearning in Jesus' lament over Jerusalem. "O Jerusalem, Jerusalem, thou that killest the prophets, and stonest them which are sent unto thee, how often would I have gathered thy children together, even as a hen gathereth her chickens under her wings, and ye would not!" (Matt. 23:37). God most certainly will have His will upon His enemies, but it seems not certainly His will that they be His enemies. "As I live . . . I have no pleasure in the death of the wicked; but that the wicked turn from his way and live: turn ye, turn ye from your evil ways; for why will ye die, O house of Israel?" (Ezek. 33:11). Peter attributes the supposed delay in Jesus' return to God's unwillingness "that any should perish" and His desire "that all should come to repentance" (2 Pet. 3:9).

Whether God's desires can ultimately be frustrated is a thorny theological issue. Yet it seems we may very well think so from these cries of wounded love. How otherwise could the Son of God have been "a man of sorrows, and acquainted with grief" than if His desire for the good of those He came to save could have been resisted and His redeeming purpose toward them have been by them rejected (Isa. 53:3)? We may be sure it is no inferior theology that takes the truths of Scripture as they come, allowing full force to the plain statements of Scripture about the mind of God as expressive of the way God means us to think about Him. The Man of Sorrows was expressing the mind of His Father when He grieved over those who received Him not. His countenance showed His love for the eager young ruler who came to Him seeking eternal life, and surely also His sadness when the wealthy youth would not sell all and follow Him (Mark 10:21).

Only once in Scripture was someone commanded not to grieve visibly over extreme human loss unrelated to divine judgment. That this instance was meant to be regarded as unnatural and exceptional is clear from its purpose as a sign to Israel. That it would require an emotional control well beyond normal powers is indicated by the emphatic detail of the command.

> Son of man, behold, I take away from thee the desire of thine
> eyes with a stroke: yet neither shalt thou mourn nor weep, nei-
> ther shall thy tears run down. Forbear to cry, make no mourn-
> ing for the dead, bind the tire of thine head upon thee, and put
> on thy shoes upon thy feet, and cover not thy lips, and eat not
> the bread of men. (Ezek. 24:16–17)

How starkly simple is the description of the event and Ezekiel's
obedient response. "So I spake unto the people in the morning:
and at even my wife died; and I did in the morning as I was commanded" (24:18). The prophet's highest desire, for God, was sorely
tested in a manner meant to appear extraordinary. The poignancy
of the description suggests that God was requiring of His prophet
a behavior in striking contrast to what He has affirmed generally
as natural and right in crushing deprivation.

For our reassurance on this point we have the very human example
of Abraham, who having lost the desire of his eyes, made elaborate
plans "to mourn for Sarah, and to weep for her" (Gen. 23:2). We
have also the Lord's own example. Jesus did not tell the grieving
sisters to stop weeping for Lazarus. He joined them in their tears.

It seems clear that if God can grieve over human loss, we may do
so also. The reverse is no less obvious. If God can rejoice, so may
we, and with His blessing. Jesus said that with the gift of His
Person comes also the gift of His joy (John 15:11). He told His
disciples that though they would sorrow, their sorrow would eventually "be turned into joy" (John 16:20). Joy would be for them
a sustaining possession as well as an anticipated delight, for they
possessed His promise of joy to come and would soon possess the
indwelling Source of the promise.

The "joy of the Lord" was the strength of Israel (Neh. 8:10).
An exuberant grateful delight was the prescribed atmosphere of

worship for Israel at the great religious feasts (Deut. 12:7, 12; Neh. 12:43). The psalmist repeatedly speaks of coming into the presence of God with gladness of heart. God approves high spirits at those times when He is honored with thanksgiving and praise. Yet it is heartening also to know there is biblical warrant for rejoicing on other occasions as well—at a wedding, at the long-awaited birth of a child, after a victory in battle, for the restoration of health, for the recovery of a lost coin. Scripture justifies emotional responses to what I have called the rhythms of life.

It remains for us to consider how what has been said about the value of our lesser desires and resultant feelings can stand against the call to personal sacrifice in the Christian life. To carry forward our vindication of emotional highs and lows now requires that we examine the nature of Christian self-denial and of the self to be denied.

THE SACRIFICED SELF

A body hast thou prepared me. . . . Lo, I come . . . to do thy will, O God.

Hebrews 10:5–7

13

THE DENIED SELF

"If any man will come after me, let him deny himself, and take up his cross, and follow me." So said the Lord to His disciples (Matt. 16:24). He went so far as to declare, "If any man come to me, and hate not his father, and mother, and wife, and children, and brethren, and sisters, yea, and his own life also, he cannot be my disciple" (Luke 14:26). Jesus evidently was speaking comparatively, for there was nothing of ill will in His tender regard for His own earthly mother while He was about His Father's business. His meaning surely was that the love of God must precede the lesser loves so entirely as to appear to eclipse them altogether.

That it does not eclipse them altogether, or even at all, should be clear by now from our consideration of the Second Commandment, in which Jesus commanded the love of one's neighbor as oneself. Jesus by His own example interpreted His high standard of self-denial so as not to exclude other legitimate loves but rather to elevate them in importance and dignity. Jesus was "moved with compassion" at the sight of a crowd (Mark 6:34) but also "loved Martha, and her sister, and Lazarus" (John 11:5). He showed a caring regard for the humbler objects of creation—birds and flowers and sheep. As His Father "so loved the world," so did He and came to redeem mankind and with it the rest of what He had made (Rom. 8:19–23).

Likewise though spiritual concerns were paramount in His ministry, they did not dominate to the exclusion of physical considerations. On one occasion Jesus called His disciples "apart into a desert place" to "rest a while," only to encounter a seeking multitude, which as the day drew toward evening required food. In his interrupting the disciples' rest to teach the people, the priority of the spiritual was maintained. In His healing the people and satisfying their hunger, the importance of the physical was established. In the preferring of others' needs over His own and of divine purposes over human, a triple-tiered hierarchy of loves was exemplified, one in which values are rightly scaled and no legitimate good is omitted.

The least love, of oneself, yields as necessary to the higher loves. The occasions on which it must yield are occasions of self-denial. The self's readiness to leave its earthly desires unfulfilled for the sake of God's purposes is the attitude of self-denial that Jesus said is essential to discipleship. That nothing of final importance will be lost by such yielding, and that much indeed will be gained, is the attitude of faith that reinforces and sweetens self-denial.

The question of self-denial returns us to what has been already said of the self. Scripture gives us a split view of the self. Our total created self is to be respected as the special handiwork of God. It is not to be dishonored or disparaged. Every person born is a divine masterwork, craftsmanly formed so as to reflect with his own special distinctness the glory and goodness of his Creator. The fact that the original plan of the Creator has been obscured by the fall in no way diminishes the value of the general outline still resident in humanity and progressively realized in the committed Christian. This is the affirmable self, the object of the Creator's original intent and present redeeming purpose. "The Lord," says the psalmist, "will perfect that which concerneth me," adding a prayer: "forsake not the works of thine own hands" (138:8). Paul urges the informed believer who disdains the scruples of his less-enlightened brother concerning meat offered to idols, "Destroy not him with thy meat, for whom Christ died. . . . For meat destroy not the work of God" (Rom. 14:15, 20). In his redeemed state he is doubly a work of God.

Concerning this creaturely self, it may be said that I dishonor God when I dishonor myself. Paul warns that those who engage in sexual perversion dishonor themselves as well as their Creator (Rom. 1:24). James speaks of the incongruity of blessing God and with same mouth "cursing men, which are made after the similitude of God" (3:9–10). The man who prays with his head covered or the woman who prays uncovered "dishonoureth" his or her "head" (1 Cor. 11:4–5), "head" referring to the dignity of the ruling authority but also to that of the person himself. To disregard or diminish the honor God has conferred on His chief work, even in its unredeemed state, is an act of bold contempt.

But when we refer to our moral selves, our "hearts," we cannot affirm without qualification their goodness. Our inherited sinful self now comes into the picture. Scripture speaks generally of the heart of fallen man as "deceitful above all things, and desperately wicked" (Jer. 17:9). Jesus said that "from within, out of the heart," proceeds an array of sinful possibilities, of evil thoughts and behaviors (Mark 7:21). It is true that good can come from a God-impressed heart. Concerning salvation we are told that "with the heart man believeth unto righteousness" (Rom. 10:10). A yielded heart may be "perfect with the Lord" (1 Kings 15:3), truly centered on His will. Such a heart is however the exception (15:3). From time to time there were those in Israel who "set their hearts to seek the Lord" (2 Chron. 11:16), but the greater number "set their heart on their iniquity" (Hosea 4:8).

Because of the duality of what the Scripture says about man, we must be careful to explain what we mean when we refer to the self. The entrance of sin into the world infected every subsequent human being at the center, sparing none of his powers. All that is embraced in the concept of the self was affected when it became corrupted at the center. Ever since then, the battle for the self between God and Satan has been a battle for the heart. "My son, give me thine heart," said the father in Proverbs, recognizing that to possess the heart is to possess all.

In general Christian usage the "self" designates what Paul refers to as the "flesh," the inherited sin nature, the "old man" God intends to be suppressed by the "new." When we speak of someone as selfish, self-centered, or self-willed, it is not his created self with all its possibilities but the inherited sin-corrupted self we have in mind. It stands against the work of the Holy Spirit. It must be crucified "with the affections and lusts" and its "works" must be displaced by "the fruit of the Spirit" (Gal. 5:19–24). This self rules the unredeemed. When Paul writes of depraved "lovers of their own selves, covetous, boasters, proud, blasphemers," and so forth, he has the inherited self in mind, sin driven, corrupted in the extreme (2 Tim. 3:2).

This self is radically adverse to true self-interest. A self-serving attitude is a self-isolating attitude, shutting off real love. A self-indulgent lifestyle is an empty existence, not a life path worthy of the name. A self-centered outlook is a self-bounded outlook, hardly an outlook at all. We cannot allow this sin-depraved self any measure of respect. It is the stubborn root of our continuing sinfulness, the ever-active agent of our spiritual defeat, the moral cancer that must be kept in remission and remains to be destroyed.

So what is the self we must deny in order to follow our God? It is not the sin-ridden unredeemed part of us we are told to "put off" and "reckon" dead (Eph. 4:22; Rom. 6:11). In the truest sense, Christian self-denial is not "denying all ungodliness and worldly lusts" (Titus 2:12). It is a rendering back of the created, redeemed self to its rightful Owner, a surrender of its rule and its ownership. Notice Paul's concern to maintain a distinction between the self as the work of God and that about the self which is still subject to sin: "I know that in me (that is, in my flesh,) dwelleth no good thing" (Rom. 7:18). He qualifies carefully so as not to be misunderstood. Paul was more than his flesh.

Christian self-denial, the subject of the next chapter, returns God's weakened handiwork to Him, acknowledging His right of ownership, His prerogative to do with it as He chooses. When I pledge my "all for Jesus," I am yielding back to Him something He has declared of great value—"all my being's ransomed powers"—a value to be enhanced by His rule.

14

CHRISTIAN SELF-DENIAL

A life of self-denial then is required of all Christians. In addition, special acts of self-denial are required of us from time to time. These are not identical for all Christians. God has different jobs and job descriptions for His different servants. He has different aspects of His Person to be reflected in different life roles and situations.

The reflection of His Person in a particular way may demand a special focus in one life whereas it may require an unusual breadth and flexibility in another. An instructor in a Christian school may be asked to relinquish his classroom duties in order to serve in a wider administrative role, leaving behind what he loves most and feels he does best. An administrator may be summoned back to teaching to fill a particular need after having been settled in a management position. In either case, an immediate need or newly recognized abilities may have indicated a different direction of service from what was prompted by personal desire. Often the direction of God's will parallels personal interests and desires, but sometimes not.

What is constant in all Christian living is a willingness to deny lesser desires in order to fulfill the highest of all desires, the approval of God. The desire for God's approval manifests the highest of all loves, the love of God. It prefers God's interests above all others. It also places the good of others above one's own.

The possibilities of self-denial are as numerous as the things of value a person can care about. Such things need not be bad in themselves. The fact that God may ask some to forgo the daily joys of family and friends for His sake is not to say these relationships are trivial. The fact of their great value—that they are so strongly affirmed in Scripture—is what makes their forsaking especially meaningful. Abraham was asked to sacrifice "the son whom thou lovest" for the sake of a higher love (Gen. 22:2). Peter was called to leave his fishing, not his lying and cursing. He was called to forsake his livelihood for the sake of a better one (Matt. 4:19; John 21:15–19). His crisis of choice, like Abraham's, was between differing legitimate loves, not between the good and the not good, the worthy and the worthless. Catching fish is less consequential than catching men.

There can be no question about the ranking of joys in the mind of the inspired musician of Psalm 137. He treasured his skill in music. His ability to sing and accompany himself on a harp was a cherished possession. It may have had much to do with his self-identity, with his sense of who as a person he was. Yet his care for his music-making was as nothing compared to his care for God. "If I forget thee, O Jerusalem, let my right hand forget her cunning. If I do not remember thee, let my tongue cleave to the roof of my mouth; if I prefer not Jerusalem above my chief joy" (Ps. 137:5–6). He would sooner have lost his skills in playing and singing than have forgotten the place of his God. Surely his music was a high and worthy love, implanted by the Creator along with musical gifts of a high order. It was an undeniable good, blessed of God and enacted in the composing and performing of his beautiful hymn. But it was unthinkable to him that it could take precedence over the divine author and subject of his playing. All his music could mean to him must give way to his "chief joy." He knew how to rank his values. He is an example for us of the spirit of self-denying submission.

The Lord's earthly life is our highest example of self-denial as a life purpose. The Savior accepted the diminishing of what was due Him—the honor and prerogatives of deity—"for the joy that was set before him," knowing that what He had relinquished would return to Him with added value (Heb. 12:2). He said that His coming to redeem mankind was a personal mission like that of a merchant finding a "pearl of great price" or of a man finding a field with buried treasure, each selling all he had to take possession of it (Matt. 13:44–46). The deprivation, though keenly felt, had gainful purpose.

A Christian settled in life may be called upon by God to narrow his life in some way so as to give it a more productive focus. He may be asked to give up something he cares greatly about in order to follow a particular life path laid out for him in the will of God. Just as a woman may need to leave the home area she loves to marry the man she loves, so a follower of Christ may need to leave the small community and rural landscape he enjoys to serve God in the city, or even leave forever his native country to serve God in a foreign land. A young couple may have to accept a primitive lifestyle to serve as missionaries in an undeveloped country. A corporate executive may need to relinquish a six-figure salary in midlife to prepare to preach. A certain life calling may require a concentration of purpose that leaves little time for a hobby or a holiday. It may keep a family thousands of miles from relatives and friends. Such choices are all the more difficult because they

Christian Self-Denial

are between lesser and greater goods, not between the intrinsically good and bad.

It follows that what is excluded in God's will for one believer may be required in His will for another, or the reverse. The Lord told Peter, with John standing by, that he would have a difficult death. "What shall this man do?" responded Peter, referring to John. The Lord replied, "What is that to thee? follow thou me" (John 21:18–22). A natural death, though denied to a faithful Peter, may have been willed by God for a faithful John. A martyr's death would therefore be right and gainful for Peter though not necessarily for John. To court martyrdom, for John or even Peter, would have been wrong. Peter should not be envious of the easier death of John, if such it was to be. John should not covet the more spectacular death promised for Peter.

Furthermore, what is mandated for certain believers in certain situations may be a matter of choice for others. There are voluntary acts of self-denial that God warmly approves, that arise from "doing the will of God from the heart" (Eph. 6:6). Certain offerings provided for Israel were offerings of "free will," gifts of gratitude beyond the required tithe of harvest and herd. Similarly a Christian family may decide to limit its Christmas spending for one another in order to help a poor family and leave behind a testimony for Christ. A Christian may make a generous gift to his church simply from a thankful heart for an answer to prayer. He may decide on his own to limit or modify his life in a certain way to improve what he is and does for the Lord. He may cut back on his eating to support his health or on his late hours to increase his alertness and physical energies. He may prefer public transportation to driving his car for the sake of witnessing opportunities. He may avoid evidences of wealth or educational advantage in order to connect more easily with people without these assets. Such

-91-

initiatives need not have originated in a divine imperative or, once decided, have to continue through life. They need not be backed by a vow. They may come simply and momentarily from a heart overflowing with love for God and for those God loves.

What is so impressive about Paul is this very thing—his willingness to deny himself goods generally approved by God in consideration of the higher purposes of his life and the desires that drove them. The hierarchy of loves was operable in Paul to an extraordinary degree. In 1 Corinthians 7 Paul insists on the goodness of marriage. Yet he recommends a condition he has adopted for himself. Discipleship in especially urgent and stressful times may favor the unmarried condition for those who can handle it, since they can serve their God with undivided interest. Paul says he has the same right as other apostles to be married and "lead about . . . a wife" (1 Cor. 9:5), but he thinks it is best for the singular strenuous ministry to which he has been called that he remain unencumbered by marriage obligations, and he suggests that those like him follow his example (1 Cor. 7:1, 6–33). It is interesting that elsewhere Paul requires of a local-church leader that he be a settled family man (1 Tim. 3:2; Titus 1:6). So it is still good that a man not live alone (Gen. 2:18), but it is also good that Paul, the pioneer missionary and apostle to the Gentiles, be able to move about freely without the responsibilities of marriage.

In 1 Corinthians Paul takes an identical stance on a second issue. The eating of marketplace meat from animals offered to idols is entirely innocent but can be troubling to some believers whose conscience rebukes them because of its association with idolatry. Paul says that if his food choices endanger the spiritual stability of a fellow believer, "I will eat no flesh while the world standeth" (1 Cor. 8:13). When writing to the Roman Christians on the issue, he treats it in the context of loves. "If thy brother be grieved with thy meat, now walkest thou not charitably" (Rom. 14:15). Paul allows that eating high-quality food is a legitimate good. But one must not let his "good be evil spoken of" (Rom. 14:16). "It is good neither to eat flesh, nor to drink wine, nor any thing whereby thy brother stumbleth, or is offended, or is made weak" (Rom. 14:21). Lesser goods must be valued beneath greater goods if they are to retain for the Christian their goodness and legitimacy.

In 1 Corinthians 10, Paul sets out his ministry as an example of what he is urging. He has a right to be supported by the churches he is nurturing, and indeed the churches have a responsibility to support him; but instead he will provide for himself. He will serve without their material help in order to deprive his accusers of any grounds for questioning his motives. His ministry to the new converts is driven not by self-will or conducted for self-benefit but constrained by a sense of obligation laid on him by God. His payment—the only reward he will take from them—is their obedience to his message, which he must carry to the world honorably and as well as he can. Here Paul seems to be saying he would have been within the will of God had he burdened himself less than he has done for the success of his ministry. He will continue providing for himself and for those with him without the help of the churches even though he need not do so.

Are there any instances in Scripture, other than the example of the Lord, of the ranking of goods and of their correspondent loves greater than these of Paul? Lesser loves are subject to higher loves, not just coldly in logically ordered ranks in some ethical system but fervently from the heart. Here is true voluntary self-denial, practically purposed and heartfelt, with due recognition of the genuine value and rightness for others of what is being denied to oneself. How different it is from a staged self-deprivation contemptuous of natural goods and normal desires affirmed by God.

Prideful self-deprivation, like all paraded spiritual attitudes and exercises, exalts rather than denies the carnal self. It is an expression of self-will emphatically condemned by God (Col. 2:23).

Let us be fully aware that self-loathing is not the core of Christian self-denial. Paul's sorrow for his actions before his conversion, contempt for his worldly credentials, and gripping sense of unworthiness must not be confused with a pietistic reveling in self-degradation. His reference to himself as the chief of sinners uniquely undeserving of God's grace was not a self-demeaning value judgment on the product of that grace (1 Tim. 1:15). In Paul an extraordinary modesty coexisted with an extraordinary sense of the importance of his life to the work he had been given to do and of his value as a cherished child of God. Paul was not only a servant of the churches he founded but also their father and nursing mother (1 Cor. 3:2; 4:15; 9:19). He was both "bondslave" to His Redeemer and "joint-heir" with the Creator of all things (Rom. 1:1; 8:17). He, like Jacob, understood well he was "not worthy of the least of all the mercies" shown him by God, but relentlessly affirmed his life in Christ (Gen. 32:10; 2 Tim. 1:12).

Self-denial then bears no resemblance to self-denigration and self-rejection. To question the wisdom of God in having shaped and styled me as He has is an act of rebellion. To dwell on my failures—my misshaping of what God has done in my life—is a mark of spiritual defeat, if not indeed of spiritual pride, misconstruing self-degradation as a Christian virtue. Self-devaluing in this mode is a disfiguring of what God has made. It takes exception to His work, denying the value He has placed upon it and the efficacy of His ongoing purposes concerning it. "Shall the thing formed say to him that formed it, Why hast thou made me thus?" (Rom. 9:20). Self-denial, for the Christian, is not the negative, self-shriveling mode of life that some have made it to be but a positive, joyous, affirmative thing. It is a wise choice among alternatives in consideration of what is best for God, for others, and therefore ultimately also for oneself.

We may conclude then that the ordering principle of Christian self-denial is the right ranking of loves. Though the specifics to be denied will vary among individual callings, the ranking itself does not change. Nor does the spiritual principle that one never relinquishes his own good when he subordinates his good to a higher. Paul could take heart from the Lord's declaration to His disciples, "He that loseth his life for my sake shall find it" (Matt. 10:39). Found it he surely has, for lose it he surely did.

15

THE OFFERED SELF

Self-denial in the strictest sense is not a forsaking of the sin-governed old nature. The "old man," as Paul calls it, is defeated, "the body of sin . . . destroyed," when we come to Christ for salvation (Rom. 6:6). Though we are warned to guard against its continuing activity, it is yet to be reckoned dead (Rom. 6:11). It is a corpse to be cast aside. This unredeemed nature is not what God wants from us as a gift to Him. It figures not at all in Christian self-denial. It is the regenerated self God desires of us—"the new man, which after God is created in righteousness and true holiness" (Eph. 4:22–24).

This yielding of the self, the regenerated self, to God has nothing to do with the diminishing of the self and its assimilation into a spiritual otherness sought in pagan mysticism. Christian self-yielding raises selfhood to what God originally meant it to be and places the self at His disposal. It takes what God has accomplished and returns it to Him as a gift. As an attitude of life, it assents to God's restorative work and responds to it cooperatively. It shows the subordination of lesser loves to greater that defines the spiritual life. God's creative work elevates its objects, and we offer Him the best of us so He can raise it more. When we recognize this vitalizing truth, we are prepared to understand Christian self-denial as self-offering.

Our great example of self-denial as self-offering is the Son of God. Christ presented to the Father not a sin-ridden self, for He had none such. A perfect nature was required in sacrifice for the sins of mankind. His choice was not between good and evil alternatives but between genuine goods—the glory rightfully His and "the joy that was set before him" (Heb. 12:2). His act of self-denial was not a rejection of Satan's tawdry kingdom for the Father's rule but a choosing between viable goods to which He was entitled. He would relinquish for a time His position at the right hand of the Father in order to repair His creation and undo the work of the Devil. The personal cost was immense. Measureless self-deprivation was for Him the price of measureless gain.

So it is that our self-offering, though primarily a grateful response of love and duty to our God, is also a gainful exchange in which lesser desires give way to greater, and value yielded becomes value added. We resign to our Redeemer something He desires and deserves and then live in a condition of blessing, a position of privilege and opportunity in which His gifts can come most richly into play and life possibilities be most fully realized. Meanwhile, we enjoy His fellowship, approval, and even honor.

Jesus encouraged His would-be followers to count the cost before answering His call, knowing, though the cost of discipleship would to many seem staggering, that even pragmatic considerations would show the greater cost of not following Him. The loss in following Him would appear trivial—indeed no loss at all—when compared with the benefit. When we follow Christ in self-denial, we can share His joy, assured that any seeming losses will yield eternal gain.

The gift of ourselves to God is also a gift to those whom God would have us serve—to "all men," but "especially unto . . . the household of faith" (Gal. 6:10). Paul said of the Macedonians that they "first gave their own selves to the Lord, and unto us by the will of God" (2 Cor. 8:5). From "their deep poverty" came their generous contribution to the distressed Jerusalem church (2 Cor. 8:2). Paul represented his own ministry to them as an offering: "Yea, and if I be offered upon the sacrifice and service of your faith, I joy, and rejoice with you all" (Phil. 2:17). Just as to love God preeminently means to love others next, so to give ourselves unreservedly to God is to do so also to others. John puts it pointedly: "He that loveth not his brother whom he hath seen, how can he love God whom he hath not seen?" (1 John 4:20). Within the hierarchy of loves is sacrificial devotion to God but also to my brother and neighbor.

In Romans 12:1 Paul depicts Christian discipleship in the context of the Jewish sacrificial ordinances. "I beseech you therefore, brethren, by the mercies of God, that ye present your bodies a living sacrifice, holy, acceptable unto God, which is your reasonable service." Paul's Jewish readers would have been well acquainted with the sacrificial offerings required in the Mosaic law. Unblemished animals of specified kinds and genders were brought to be slain by worshipers assisted by the priests. The presentation of the slain animal stood for the presentation of the offerer to God.

Those presented for sacrifice in Paul's meaning are of course not animals but persons, and the sacrificial act is from the "voluntary will" of the offered object itself (Lev. 1:3). The result paradoxically is "a living sacrifice," willingly yielding up its life but living on in temple service. As Christ offered Himself in sacrifice and thereafter lives as our High Priest, so His followers are both sacrifice and priest and after their self-sacrifice continue to serve.

Paul may have had a particular instance in mind. After the exodus the Lord told Moses, "Sanctify unto me all the firstborn, whatsoever openeth the womb among the children of Israel, both of man and of beast: it is mine" (Exod. 13:2). The firstborn of the animals were to be slain in sacrifice, but the human firstborn were to be redeemed (Exod. 13:13). They were redeemed by a substitute that would remain alive and belong to the Lord in a special way.

After the construction of the tabernacle, the Lord gave Moses more exact instructions.

> Thou shalt bring the Levites before the tabernacle of the congregation: and thou shalt gather the whole assembly of the children of Israel together: and thou shalt bring the Levites before the Lord: and the children of Israel shall put their hands upon the Levites: and Aaron shall offer the Levites before the Lord for an offering of the children of Israel, that they may execute the service of the Lord. . . . And after that shall the Levites go in to do the service of the tabernacle of the congregation: and thou shalt cleanse them, and offer them for an offering. For they are wholly given unto me from among the children of Israel; instead of such as open every womb, even instead of the firstborn of all the children of Israel, have I taken them unto me. (Num. 8:9–16)

The involuntary separation of the Levites to perform the service of the sanctuary as living sacrifices prefigured what Paul was summoning believers in Christ to do "as a reasonable service" of their own free will.

As living sacrifices, believers are said to be without blemish. They appear before God in the righteousness of Christ. They also continue to live as priests ordained to His service, actualizing in their lives the holiness that has been declared of them. In serving "the temple of the living God," they must, like the Levites, remain separate from defilement; they must "touch not the unclean thing" (2 Cor. 6:16–17). As sacrifices, they must, as required in the ceremonial laws, have salt—be savory in their personal dealings (Mark 9:50; Lev. 2:13; cf. Job 6:6). They "are unto God a sweet savour of Christ, in them that are saved, and in them that perish," to those that perish a "savour of death unto death" and to the saved a "savour of life unto life" (Eph. 5:2; 2 Cor. 2:15–16). Their lives like burnt offerings give off an aroma that is a reminder of death to the one and of life to the other.

Paul's reference to the body rather than to the self as a whole may seem odd until we remember the association being developed with animal sacrifices. The bodies of animals were the focus of the priest who inspected them before they were slain and burnt on the great altar. But beyond that, the human body is the mortal container of the self and its vehicle. The body situates the self in the world and carries out the intentions of the mind and heart. It can be an instrument of good or of evil (Rom. 6:13). Thus for Paul the presentation of the body to God is a consecration of the total human being. To offer the self to God in some vague sort of way that exempts its physical operations and manifestations is theory without practice—definitely not the same as complete commitment.

Paul had taken this step. He summed his life purpose in the wish that "Christ shall be magnified in my body, whether it be by life, or by death" (Phil. 1:20). To accomplish this purpose would be to accomplish all. To present the body as a living sacrifice meant to Paul the unreserved and irrevocable gift of the entire self to God.

At conversion God begins a work of reclamation in which a spiritually implanted "new creature" takes over the old, and "all things are become new" and "are of God" (2 Cor. 5:17–18). That the new self does not immediately replace the old, nor will entirely do so until the end of the present life, does not diminish in the least our identity as new creations of God. We are to regard ourselves as "dead indeed unto sin, but alive unto God through Jesus Christ our Lord" (Rom. 6:11), while in the meantime staying vigilant toward the old nature's continuing efforts to reassert itself.

When we recognize this vitalizing truth, we are prepared to understand self-denial as self-offering.

16

THE OFFERED LIFE

The offered self and the offered life are by nature the same act of commitment. But in actual practice the two are not always found together. It is easier to offer ourselves to God in a vague, abstract sort of way than to grant Him our life goals and daily doings. To pledge our lives to God in all mundane respects carries with it concrete specifics that cannot so easily fade in the mind. The Epistle of James makes clear that in matters of religious profession practice comes harder than theory (James 2:24–26).

What can stand in the way of the offered life is the notion that God owes each of us a normal life. This, of course, is patently false. God owes us nothing. He distributes to His creatures according to His sovereign will and good pleasure, with their good in mind along with His other purposes. Beyond that fundamental fact is the equally evident truth that no one ever born has had what can be called a truly normal life. How few are the lives given prominence in Scripture that can be said to be by any account normal. Where are the normal families in the Bible and the normal life paths of its major or even minor figures? Where is complete normalcy of life outside of Scripture? Common observation exposes the myth of a normal life. When we speak of normality in life we must do so in very approximate terms.

It is true that there is a general pattern of settled existence recognized in Scripture as something to be desired and received as a blessing from God. The prophets foretell times of national blessing when people will dwell in peace and be settled happily in families. Old men and women will move about the streets, which will ring with the sounds of children playing, with "the voice of joy, and the voice of gladness, the voice of the bridegroom, and the voice of the bride" (Zech. 8:4–5; Jer. 33:11). It is God Who "setteth the solitary in families" (Ps. 68:6), Who "maketh the barren woman to keep house, and to be a joyful mother of children" (113:9). Abraham "died in a good old age, an old man, and full of years; and was gathered to his people" (Gen. 25:8). So also, finally, did Job.

But settled conditions of life are not always available or even to be sought. "Is it a time to receive money, and to receive garments, and oliveyards, and vineyards, and sheep, and oxen, and menservants, and maidservants?" asked Elisha of his materialistic servant Gehazi (2 Kings 5:26). Paul, writing in a time of persecution with worse times to follow, advised against seeking a settled existence. "It remaineth, that both they that have wives be as though they had none; and they that weep, as though they wept not; and they that rejoice, as though they rejoiced not; and they that buy, as though they possessed not; and they that use this world, as not abusing it [as not making full use of it, NASB]" (1 Cor. 7:29–31). At such times a normal life, even approximately speaking, would be hardly possible or even desirable. Though a genuine good, such a life was not for Paul an absolute good. He was his own best example.

It is natural to recoil from the risk of an abnormal life. Probably the hardest lesson in life is learning to do without. Yet who of us, any more than David, would think it reasonable to offer to the Lord in sacrifice that which costs us nothing (2 Sam. 24:24)? Many an ambitious careerist will narrow his life to serve a ruler—a politician or a bureaucrat or a corporate executive—depriving himself and his family of an ordinary life in order to reach his material goals. Who would not narrow his life to serve a great King, though His kingdom be not of this world? Is such not our "reasonable service" (Rom. 12:1)? These are questions to ponder.

Some may draw back from the challenge of the offered life from a disrespect for what they have to offer. They may seem to themselves poorly endowed, their lives undistinguished, perhaps malformed or broken. They live day by day with a painful sense of lack. They need not think so. They are exceptionally well constituted to present their lives to God. He treasures the self-gift of those who feel low: of such as are "poor in spirit," of whom Jesus said, "Theirs is the kingdom of heaven" (Matt. 5:3), and of the "meek," who He said "shall inherit the earth" (Matt. 5:5). He will assure them they are, like all faithful followers of God, "greatly beloved" and cherished (Dan. 9:23; Mal. 3:17). He knows how to encourage His own, embarrassed and anxious about their inadequacies. "Fear not, little flock; for it is your Father's good pleasure to give you the kingdom" (Luke 12:32).

But the questioning of life worth can also arise from a not-so-admirable spirit: from resentment toward the Creator for neglecting His work. A sense of having been slighted in life can harden the heart, even of a child of God. Especially it can happen when a life-narrowing loss brings with it a continual challenge in coping. Bitterness can take possession of the mind, feelings of anger toward God for what is felt to be His faulty design of the life. The suddenly widowed or the physically disabled from birth have had ɔ call from God to limit their lives. God has limited their lives :eady. Their challenge is to accept the persons they are and to value the lives they have been given.

Scripture speaks to these hesitations in an instance already noted. It gives us the example of the man blind from birth. "Who did sin, this man, or his parents, that he was born blind?" the disciples asked the Savior. He replied, "Neither hath this man sinned, nor his parents: but that the works of God should be made manifest in him" (John 9:2–3). Here was a man who had never known an existence free of humiliating dependence upon others. His life, said Jesus, had been drastically limited for a purpose, the highest imaginable: "that the works of God should be made manifest in him." God had a positive purpose for making him as He had.

We may be sure that no one is ever born "handicapped" for God's particular use for him. Each human being is a delicately crafted masterpiece, wonderfully put together to glorify God and receive His special blessing. The Rolls-Royce firm reportedly has had a practice of not divulging the strength of the engines that power their magnificent vehicles. An awed observer in a showroom will ask, "What is the horsepower under that hood?" "It's adequate" is the answer. The implication is "adequate and much more." God similarly equips us for what He has for us to do. We have powers that are exquisitely matched to the life plans assigned us— "adequate and much more"—and also styled to our personal enjoyment. Our very limitations can add luster to our accomplishments for Him and increase our joy.

So it was that Paul accepted his limitation, his "thorn in the flesh," with the recognition that whatever God accomplished through him would be all the more remarkable and the praise of God all the greater. "Most gladly therefore will I rather glory in my infirmities," said he, "that the power of Christ may rest upon me" (2 Cor. 12:9). Paul turned a natural negative into a spiritual positive and found cause to rejoice in it. A less-than-average life situation can be accepted gratefully as a good, as an opportunity to bear special witness to the power and goodness of God. The resulting accomplishments can seem minor miracles to a baffled world.

There is special encouragement for the hesitant in a source we have already consulted: the Old Testament sacrificial ordinances. The male Levites, as we noticed, were set apart as living sacrifices, replacing the male firstborn that were to be offered to God. Among the Levites one might find all manner of variety, persons gifted and flawed in all ways imaginable. Yet the life of each of them was to be respected as an offering to the Lord. All had important functions to perform.

If we turn to the animal offerings described in the Mosaic law, we read that all sacrificed animals were to be without blemish—all, that is, except one. This offering was to be voluntary, an offering "unto the Lord" on the occasion of "a singular vow." It needed not be of an animal, but if it were, the condition of the animal did not determine its suitability. The animal need not be flawless. Whatever its state, it could not be exchanged for a worse or a better. The giver "shall not alter it, nor change it, a good for a bad, or a bad for a good: and if he shall at all change beast for beast, then it and the exchange thereof shall be holy" (Lev. 27:2, 9–10). The offering was to be presented "as is."

Such is the case when we offer ourselves and our lives to God. We do not weigh our natural assets and liabilities. We do not assess our usefulness to God—how He will be advantaged or disadvantaged by accepting our service. We simply give God what He wants: *ourselves*, the sum total of the materials of His handiwork in ourselves and in our lives, plusses and minuses together. We present ourselves confidently and gratefully in the spirit of the Mosaic "singular vow," each life a unique, approved gift, recognized and valued by God. We pledge ourselves to God as we are, as a bride does to her husband, as a groom does to his bride, "for better, for worse, for richer, for poorer, in sickness, and in health, to love and to cherish, till death,"—a death, however, which will never "us part."

And if the life we have to offer is a wretched confusion, shattered by blows from the world and reduced to a sin-stricken rubble? Then we make from the fragments of that life an altar on which to offer what is left of our poor selves. "An altar of earth thou shalt make unto me," said the Lord to His people, adding "in all places where I record my name I will come unto thee, and I will bless thee" (Exod. 20:24). We ourselves, formed of the dust of the ground, can be that altar of earth as well as the sacrifice placed upon it.

It has been well said that everyone has a "past." In shaping any life, the Lord has only imperfect materials. He is known for His skill in reclamation. "I the Lord build the ruined places, and plant that that was desolate," declared the Lord to Israel through His prophet Ezekiel (36:36). "I will restore to you the years that the locust hath eaten," promised Jehovah to a people in revolt from Him concerning future blessing (Joel 2:25). The Lord can masterfully refashion a broken life into something of strength and beauty, even redeeming somehow and to an extent the years that have been lost. So He did with the once degenerate slave trader John Newton, later revered preacher and writer of beloved hymns. So he did supremely with Paul. From the example of the apostle himself—midlife convert, fierce opponent of Christ—we may be sure it is never too late to offer a life, so unpromising a life as his, to God.

We confront here the issue of self-acceptance. There is a sense in which self-acceptance is fatal to the work of God in a life. It stands in the way of salvation. It blocks spiritual growth. Self-acceptance as self-satisfaction—contentment with what one is and what one has done minus God—is responsible for spiritual failure and life tragedy. It is the damning sin of the rich man in Luke 12, who thought that by heaping up wealth he could satisfy his soul. It is the impoverishing sin of believers who persuade themselves that well enough is enough in their effort to resist sin and forward the work of God in their lives. Scripture condemns those "at ease in Zion." Self-acceptance in this sense is the way of spiritual decline and demise.

But there is another sense in which self-acceptance is necessary to spiritual success. To be contented with what you are because of God, with the way God has put you together and endowed you for His pleasure and your good, with your life as He has ordained and ordered it—such self-acceptance is the grateful attitude of spiritual victory. Discontent with one's condition in this sense is a complaint against God. It brought destruction on an entire generation of Israel in the Sinai desert and is as ruinous as spiritual self-satisfaction. "Woe unto him that striveth with his Maker," wrote the prophet Isaiah (45:9). Carnal discontent with oneself accompanying low spirits is a temptation comparable to carnal content with oneself accompanying high spirits. We dare not undervalue what God has given us to return as an offering to Him.

A wholesome spiritual contentment centers on a respect for the work of God in the person and life of His creature. We esteem His work in ourselves not competitively like the Pharisee who thanked God he was not as other men but like Paul in conjunction with His work in others. The apostle took special pleasure in the sharable blessings of salvation while not at all undervaluing the particular life task assigned him by God and the endowments that fitted him for it. "I am what I am," he said. In this sense of self-acceptance—appreciation for what God has done in our persons and lives in both general and distinctive ways—we cannot esteem ourselves too highly. To disesteem what God has done in us and has in mind for us is to question the wisdom and goodness of God.

We have encountered once again that two-sided truth of our self-concept. There is no self-merit that commends a sinner to God in salvation. That is the message for the unconverted. Yet there is inestimable value to every human life, a value progressively realized by the power of God in sanctification. The parable of the talents is a warning to every Christian to keep well in mind the importance of what God has wrought in him lest he dishonor God by discounting and neglecting the qualities with which he has been entrusted (Matt. 25:14–30).

In his last epistle Paul calls to mind the "unfeigned faith" that is in Timothy, "which dwelt first in thy grandmother Lois, and thy mother Eunice," and reminds Timothy to "stir up the gift of God, which is in thee by the putting on of my hands" (2 Tim. 1:5–6). There are good things in Timothy that must not be depreciated and neglected but must be offered to God in service.

The Christian offers his life to God knowing that whatever is given to God comes back enlarged and enriched to the giver. Yet there is an even more consequential benefit. To yield one's life to God, placing it in His hands to work His wonders with it, is to escape the tyranny of anxious desire. No longer can fear of failure, regret for unfulfilled hopes, gnawing frustrations, weaken the spirit and raise questions about the goodness of God. One can rest confident that the great fashioner of lives will do His work to the utmost perfection, satisfying Himself while blessing us also.

A husband, amused by his wife's habit at restaurants of preferring his menu choice to her own and asking him to split with her, replied to her latest request with mock exasperation: "Sweetheart, if you let me order for you, you'll get what you want." The husband's teasing reply is also our assurance from God when we put our lives at His disposal. There need be no hesitancy, for if we let Him order for us, we'll get what we want. "To what purpose is this waste?" asks an incredulous world (Matt. 26:8). The surrendered child of God knows better. Experience has taught him that God's choices are better than his own.

The self we offer God is the total life, including the rich complexities of the emotions. We shall see how the full play of the emotional life is part of the offering. The great Composer of our natures is also the great Conductor of our lives, managing their rhythms as in passages of a splendid symphony, ordering the performance toward a wise and wonderful end. And if the feelings have been bludgeoned by life? We can bring the damaged machinery to God and offer it with the rest of ourselves to the Master Technician to do with as He pleases. What the Master Technician chooses to do with it will be good. For the Master Technician happens to be also the Master Composer and Conductor. He produces rare music with flawed instruments given to Him. The music of the Maestro revives in self-offering and can surge exquisitely even during struggle and pain.

THE EXULTING SELF

And thou shalt rejoice in every good thing which the Lord thy God hath given unto thee.

Deuteronomy 26:11

17

ON MY HIGH PLACES

Can conscientious Christians be subject to instabilities of mood? Can they have severe highs and lows? Does not a mature spirituality level the pitch and roll of the emotions? This is the question that has driven our inquiry concerning the nature of the self and its desires. We can now at last begin to close the circle concerning what Scripture has to tell us about our emotional variations, drawing upon the discussion thus far.

Let us keep in mind that Scripture does not mandate an unflappable emotional norm. Paul's "spirit was stirred in him" when he saw the idolatry of Corinth. The psalmist said, "I remembered God, and was troubled: I complained [lamented], and my spirit was overwhelmed." To which he added, "Thou holdest mine eyes waking: I am so troubled that I cannot speak" (Ps. 77:3–4). His thoughts had turned toward the Lord with the result that his feelings were profoundly stirred. The Lord Himself was "troubled in spirit" by the thought that "one of you shall betray me" (John 13:21). His disciples on occasions before had witnessed His anger and grief.

Emotional urgency is implied in Naomi's words to Ruth concerning Boaz, who was then inquiring about the legalities of

their marrying: "The man will not be in rest, until he have finished the thing this day." Ruth would have her own feelings to
manage: "Sit still, my daughter, until thou know how the matter will fall" (Ruth 3:18). Pressured desire in Ruth and Boaz,
directed by the Lord, gave them a place in the genealogical line
of the Savior. Who would question that good can come from
agitation of mind?

On the other end of the emotional spectrum, instances abound
of joyous excitement in Scripture and without evidence of divine
displeasure. God appears to delight in our delight. It pleases Him
to make "all things work together for good" in a life, to satisfy "the
desires of thine heart" (Rom. 8:28; Ps. 37:4). He will "freely give
us all things" (Rom. 8:32). He sanctifies with His presence those
times of special joy—a wedding, the birth of a child, the second
birth of a soul. "The steps of a good man are ordered by the Lord:
and he delighteth in his way" (Ps. 37:23).

So it may seem strange to think it necessary to justify feelings of
delight. Surely there is exuberance aplenty in the Psalms, in the
Song of Songs, in the promise of blessings in the prophets, in the
rapturous passages of the epistles of Paul. David, looking back
on his life, showed exhilaration when he said that God made his
feet nimble and set them skipping (and climbing), raising his delight (and position of advantage) to the heights. "He maketh my
feet like hinds' feet: and setteth me upon my high places" (2 Sam.
22:34; see also Hab. 3:19). David's fighting days were over. He was
speaking of his mind states as well as his present circumstances.
We recall that John the Baptist's father, Zacharias, was promised
"joy and gladness" at the birth of a son, at which "many shall rejoice" (Luke 1:14). The gospel is itself "glad tidings" (Acts 13:32;
Rom. 10:15). At the return of the prodigal son, "they began to be
merry" (Luke 15:24).

The issue nevertheless came up after Levi's dinner when Jesus was questioned by the Pharisees about His disciples' festive behavior. He quickly settled it, replying that His presence alone was reason enough for them to "eat and drink" and be in good spirits. In time He would "be taken away from them," and then they would have reason to "fast" (Luke 5:33–35). In doing so, observed G. Campbell Morgan, the Lord was defending "the right of His people to be merry."[1] This "right" belonged to the children of the Bridegroom. It needed defending against the severe religionists of His day, and sometimes has needed it since.

Still, biblical evidence for the legitimacy of high spirits is so strong that the issue for most of us seems hardly necessary to raise. Scripture does not defend our right to be merry with a "Well, I suppose so" or a "Perhaps sometimes," but with a resounding "Yes." "It was meet that we should make merry, and be glad," said the prodigal's father to the censorious elder brother, having ordered a sumptuous banquet on his return (Luke 15:32).

Yet put another way, this right to elevated feelings can come under strong suspicion. High spirits ordinarily come from thoughts of well being, from a sense that certain things about us and our lives are "right" and going well. Dare we think so? Flawed, stumbling creatures that the best of us are, can we think it ever justifiable to feel good about ourselves and about the way our lives in a fallen world are tending? How can we be uplifted by such trivial delights as, say, a surprise party, a dozen roses brought to the door, a good set of semester grades, a refreshing round of golf, a job promotion, when there is so much wrong with the world and so much wrong in ourselves? Are we not of the "poor in spirit" who "mourn"—sober souls burdened with the sin of the world and their own shortcomings? Are not high spirits, though tolerated in Scripture, inconsistent with serious spirituality and bedrock theological truth? Is not a Christian who rejoices in his condition and enjoys pleasant moments a walking contradiction?

Jesus said that "the poor in spirit" who "mourn" should consider themselves "blessed," favorably situated. They should "rejoice" in their condition, even when the world persecutes them and regards them quite otherwise (Matt. 5:3–4, 10–12). They should do so because of what they possess in this life and what they will inherit in the next. Jesus spoke to their anxiety about their personal status, assuring them that it was indeed good and would improve with time. He said that believers in acute distress at the time of His return were to "lift up your heads; for your redemption draweth nigh" (Luke 21:28). This grounded expectation of good yet to come is the essence of faith according to the writer of Hebrews (11:1). It is a "confidence" believers must "cast not away," for it "hath great recompense of reward" (Heb. 10:35). They must "hold fast . . . the rejoicing of the hope firm unto the end" (Heb. 3:6).

It would seem then that the poor in spirit are not poor in confidence of their present and future gain as members of the household of God and that their confidence is shown in their rejoicing. Be "glad and rejoice for ever in that which I create," said Jehovah through the prophet Isaiah. The new creation, yet to come in its fullest form, has already begun in the child of God—in the "new man, which after God is created in righteousness and true holiness" (Isa. 65:18; Eph. 4:24). He may begin rejoicing now.

Of course our present condition of life in a fallen world as pilgrims and strangers identified with the Man of Sorrows warrants low spirits at times. That we still have about us a disposition to sin and can yield to it justifies, even requires, low spirits at times of spiritual lapse. The Day of Atonement, requiring soul affliction, was necessary preparation for the Feast of Tabernacles, requiring elation, five days later. But for our down times Scripture is ready with reminders of our enviable condition in Christ, set out in terms meant to lift our spirits. "All things are for your sakes," said Paul, speaking for the One "who giveth us richly all things to enjoy" (2 Cor. 4:15; 1 Tim. 6:17).

18

PERSONAL HONOR

Evidently God means us to take pleasure in our status as His redeemed children. We sing heartily and with good reason "It is well with my soul." Still the more difficult part of our question remains: whether from considerations other than our redeemed status our spirits may justifiably rise. At this point we reach the crux of the issue.

Is it right, let us ask, to accept personal honor? The enemies of the Lord "loved the praise of men more than the praise of God" and were condemned for it (John 12:43). He said to them, "How can ye believe, which receive honour one of another, and seek not the honour that cometh from God only?" (John 5:44). Evidently seeking honor was not in itself their problem. Their problem was their seeking it from the wrong source. "Let us not be desirous of vain glory," writes Paul, making the point that seeking worldly honor is foolish as well as sinful (Gal. 5:26). This honor, we know from life as well as from Scripture, is notoriously fickle. Its most odious and deceitful form is self-flattery. We are not to accept praise from ourselves. "Let another man praise thee, and not thine own mouth; a stranger, and not thine own lips," says the inspired proverb (Prov.

27:2). "Not he that commendeth himself is approved, but whom the Lord commendeth," writes the apostle Paul (2 Cor. 10:18).

Jesus made clear that there is an honor downward from God to man that may legitimately be sought and even expected. "If any man serve me, him will my Father honour" (John 12:26). The truth appears in the Old Testament as well. Concerning the man who trusts in Him, God says through the psalmist, "I will deliver him, and honour him" (91:15). God evidently does not think it inappropriate to show His favor in this way to His own.

There is also, beyond the divinely bestowed honor, an honor legitimately rendered by man to man—an honoring that God not only permits but also requires. Jesus emphasized to the Pharisees the binding importance of the Fifth Commandment, "Honour thy father and mother," accusing them of nullifying the commandment by their rabbinical restrictions (Matt. 15:1–6). Flagrant dishonor of one's parents in the Mosaic law was a capital offense. Human honoring was important in the New Testament churches, where, said Paul, the elders were to be honored, and those who "rule well" were to "be counted worthy of double honour." It was due them just as certainly as "the labourer is worthy of his reward" (1 Tim. 5:17–18). The Thessalonians were "to know them which labour among you, and are over you in the Lord, and admonish you; and to esteem them very highly in love for their work's sake" (1 Thess. 5:12–13). In both family and church, human honor had and continues to have a divine mandate behind it.

Concerning civil society, Peter coupled the command to "fear God" with "honour the king" (1 Pet. 2:17). Obeying both commands at once is one of the more difficult challenges confronting God's people during times of ruler misconduct and moral decline. To "render to Caesar the things that are Caesar's" requires of Christians a certain honor toward ruling authorities, both good and bad. Even when disobedience to rulers is required for the sake of obeying God, honor must accompany disobedience. Peter, refusing to obey man (the Sanhedrin) rather than God, explained his refusal respectfully (Acts 5:29–32). Paul apologized to a corrupt high priest for having unwittingly reproached him (23:5). They possess degenerate minds, said Peter, who "despise government" and "are not afraid to speak evil of dignities" (2 Pet. 2:10). It is sinful to withhold honor from those to whom honor is due in the three institutions established by God: the family, the church, and civil society.

From the passage in 1 Peter just cited we learn also that there is a certain honor attached to the simple fact of being a special creation of God. "Honour all men," commands the apostle (2:17). We know this obligation also from the fact that a man can dishonor himself, acting against the dignity of his created nature, and be held accountable for it by God. Paul writes of those who "dishonour their own bodies" in gross sin against the Creator of their bodies (Rom. 1:24). Every person carries with him in the eyes of God a certain creaturely stature, and we are to respect the dignity of his essential humanity even if he does not. He bears the image of his Creator, an image that though obscured by sin cannot be entirely expunged. The psalmist spoke to this purpose when he said of man, "Thou madest him a little lower than the angels; thou crownedst him with glory and honour" (Heb. 2:7). Certainly there can be no doubt that high dignity is being claimed for this fractured masterwork of God.

There are specific dignities ascribed in Scripture to general conditions and stages of life. In the Old Testament, respect for age is associated with the fear of God. "Thou shalt rise up before the hoary head, and honour the face of the old man, and fear thy God" (Lev. 19:32). Additional recognition is due to the God-fearing elderly.

"The hoary head is a crown of glory, if it be found in the way of righteousness" (Prov. 16:31). Because of the honor required for age in Scripture, Paul instructed Timothy to "rebuke not an elder, but entreat him as a father," and yet also to "let no man" for that reason "despise thy youth" (1 Tim. 5:1; 4:12).

For youth has its proper dignity as well. A child, said the Lord, is the model citizen of the kingdom of heaven (Matt. 18:2–4; 19:13–14). To despise a child is to incur severe divine displeasure (Matt. 18:10). There is even a certain dignity to youthful love. No one can read the Song of Solomon and fail to see the praise bestowed by the lover on his beloved. "Thou art all fair, my love; there is no spot in thee" (Song of Sol. 4:7). An unmarried woman has her special dignity. A father has not done his job who has not helped his daughter come to know herself as a desirable young woman with the dignity proper to her sex. When this honor has been forcibly violated, she is "humbled," not at all in a commendable way (Deut. 22:29). Amnon, when thus humbling Tamar, was not a coworker with God (2 Sam. 13:1–20). We should know well by now in America that to humiliate someone because of his race is not to do him a spiritual service.

This general human dignity recognized in Scripture underscores the sanctity of human life in distinction from the lives of the lower animals. It underlies the delight of a family in a newborn, the exuberance of well-wishers at a wedding, the pleasure taken in other milestones of a life. It justifies the demure dignity of a bride being honored on her special day. It solemnizes a funeral and makes appropriate the memorializing of the dead. Honoring is biblically in order at such times, and the honoree would be ill tempered indeed to disdain it, though allowances must of course be granted the newborn and the deceased.

The inspired author of Proverbs writes concerning the "virtuous woman" of chapter 31, "Give her of the fruit of her hands; and let her own works praise her in the gates" (v. 31). She is not to be denied human recognition for what she has virtuously done. The woman of Bethany who poured precious ointment on the head of the Savior performed "a good work," for which she would ever be honored (Matt. 26:10, 13). An act or a life can be worthy of praise.

It seems obvious that if giving honor to another is required by the One Who Himself honors and rewards the faithful, agreeably receiving the given honor is willed of God also. It will hardly do to say that honor is all right to be given but wrong to be received. Saul was discreditably shy when he "hid himself among the stuff" to escape his anointing as Israel's king (1 Sam. 10:20–23). Later when "the Spirit of God came upon Saul," he threw off his backwardness, accepting his role as leader of God's people and performing it, at least this once, obediently and vigorously (1 Sam. 11:6). There is sin in the ungracious spurning as well as the covetous seeking of human honor and reward. God puts no premium on boorishness.

19

WORTHLESSNESS AND WORTH

Because God recognizes and rewards, we must also. Because we also recognize and reward after His example, the recipients must accept the given recognition and reward with gratitude. Yet we are still not done with our question. Is it acceptable to have feelings of well being when one is thus honored? Are high spirits justifiable at such times?

From a devout tradition noted earlier comes the belief that the more spiritual one is, the less he thinks he amounts to. One's spirituality is inversely proportional to one's self-regard. Let us examine this sincerely held belief biblically and carefully. Most certainly there is a self-abhorrence necessary in the sinner coming to God for salvation and in the sinning saint as well. Of the moral bankruptcy of the seeking sinner there can be no question, or of the impotence of a believer acting independently of God. "Without me ye can do nothing," said the Lord to His disciples the night before His crucifixion (John 15:5). We understand well that when the best of God's servants—a Job, a Daniel, or an Isaiah—confronts the blazing perfection of God's holiness, his "comeliness" will be "turned . . . into corruption" and he will retain "no strength"

(Dan. 10:8). When a simple-hearted, spiritually sensitive saint is touched by his smallness before God, by his unworthiness to be a mere object of God's attention, and makes his spiritual project the diminishing of what he calls "self," the Lord is indeed pleased by his sense of spiritual poverty and draws near in special friendship and comforting assurance.

Indeed a persistent theme of Scripture is God's respect for the humble spirit. God honors and rewards lowliness of heart, even when the honoree may doubt the rightness of the honoring and the rewarding. But it is nevertheless true that personal worthlessness does not sum up the account of the redeemed sinner in the view of God. A preoccupation with personal worthlessness keeps the focus on the "old man." It can amount to a kind of reverse pride. Wholesome self-abasement came to Isaiah from his view of God, not from long meditation on his sinfulness. The humblest imaginable of Christians, the apostle Paul, warns against a "voluntary humility"—that is, against a deliberate self-demeaning for the sake of spiritual gain (Col. 2:18).

Here again we meet the two-sided truth of man's worthlessness and his immense worth. There is nothing about the inherited, unredeemed self that counts with God for salvation or should count with us after salvation. And yet the created self is ascribed a value by God above that of the rest of His creation, a value prompting an incalculable sacrifice. When Jesus put to His disciples the question "What shall it profit a man, if he shall gain the whole world, and lose his own soul?" (Mark 8:36), He was in effect telling them to raise, not lower, their self-estimation, to accept the enormous value He had placed on their lives and on their souls.

The philosopher Blaise Pascal (1623–62) warned of twin dangers to mankind—knowing God without knowing one's own wretchedness and knowing one's own wretchedness without knowing God. The first error conduces to pride, the second to despair, sins deadly to the soul. Believers can err, and err seriously, in comparable ways: in knowing their created worth without remembering their natural moral worthlessness and in knowing their natural moral worthlessness without remembering their created worth. We who believe, as we surely must, in natural depravity must not be theologically spooked by what Scripture has to tell us of man's unregenerate meritlessness into denying his creaturely worth. The two, man's moral and creaturely worths, are not the same. We hold the biblical double view of man.

We have about us then that which should both elevate and subdue our self-estimate. We are God's treasured possession but are woefully incapable in ourselves of actualizing the value He confers and of warranting the honor He bestows. Our status is high, backed by the divine declaration of our worth, while our worthiness is low. "I am not worthy of the least of all the mercies, and of all the truth, which thou hast shewed unto thy servant," prayed the man surnamed by Jehovah "prince with God" (Gen. 32:10, 27–28). We can easily understand our unworthiness, and that should ever humble us. We can never understand our worth—a fact we must grasp by faith and acknowledge with grateful pleasure. We may accept rendered honor from our fellow humans with grateful pleasure as well.

20

Workers Together with God

This positive awareness of our condition in Christ and our personal worth is important to our Christian service. Matthew Henry, commenting on Romans 12, warns against the spiritual inertia that can result from a low regard for what we amount to in Christ. "Take heed lest under a pretense of humility and self-denial, we be slothful in laying out ourselves for the good of others. We must not say, 'I am nothing, therefore I will do nothing' but 'I am nothing in myself, and therefore I will lay out myself to the utmost in the strength of the grace of Christ."[1] F. B. Meyer, remarking on Romans 12:10, warns against "allowing ourselves to fall into a habit of self-depreciation, which is always standing back from responsibility and duty." This failure to recognize our creaturely worth can keep us from making use of what God has put into us. "We may be so sensitive to our failures, and so depreciate ourselves, as to fail to give adequate expression to the idea which God has incarnated in our constitution."[2]

Jesus made a similar point in John 15. A branch separated from the vine is a nothing, a useless nuisance. It is fit only to be "cast forth" and disposed of. A branch connected to the vine is very much a something, situated so as to perform its natural work, the production of fruit, a fruit associated in Scripture especially with joy (John 15:1–8). This reminder of their value when joined to Him was spoken by Jesus to His disciples the night before His crucifixion to comfort them in their sorrow—so that their "joy might be full" (John 15:11). Much would depend upon their abiding in Him—their joy as well as their service. Their abiding in Him would be encouraged by a clear sense of their regarded worth.

Since our accomplishments depend upon our abiding in Christ and are due to His guidance and strength, may we justifiably accept praise for them and is there a justifiable personal satisfaction in the accomplishment? Are the tasks we complete and the goals we reach really our doings in any sense such that we can legitimately be credited with them and honored for performing them? Can we properly possess feelings of satisfaction from having seen them to completion? Is it reverent even to speak of them as personal accomplishments? We are of course "unprofitable servants" in the sense that nothing we can ever do in obedience to God will improve His status in the least (Luke 17:10). But is there a sense borne out in Scripture in which our particular labors on God's behalf can be considered ours as well as His? Here we reach the most delicate part of the question raised three chapters ago. As before, we may find our answer in the example and words of the Savior.

Jesus invited the "weary and heavy laden" to accept His yoke, for, He said, "my yoke is easy, and my burden is light" (Matt. 11:30). This yoke, accepted, is both His and ours, a shared yoke. We are invited to a participatory fellowship of labor in which the divine Inviter pulls, but so must we. Without His pulling, we *could* not pull. Without our pulling, He *would* not pull—in matters, that is, whose success He ordains to depend upon our participation.

That spiritual ministry may be regarded as a cooperative effort involving the human laborer and God is clear from Paul's statement on ministerial collaboration. That one worker has planted and another has watered is no less a fact than that it is God Who "giveth the increase," for "we are," says Paul, "labourers together with God" (1 Cor. 3:7–9). The analogy is speaking not of the relative efficacy of the contributions by God and man but of a divinely granted collaboration. Each of us is invited to participate with God in God-enabled undertakings. The doubleness of the yoke is the doubleness of a two-sided truth.

The human side is the variable part, and it is a participation God not only recognizes but also has promised to honor and reward. There is in Scripture a doctrine of personal righteousness with scalable degrees recognized by God not for salvation—a point repeatedly stressed by Paul—but for heavenly reward. At the final judging of believers, when we stand for rewards, it is not our imputed righteousness that will be assessed. That is constant in all the redeemed and cannot be scaled for compensation. Imputed righteousness is by very definition unrewardable, for it is entirely gratuitous and infinite, being the righteousness of the Savior. It is instead a variable faithfulness in character and service which the Lord is "not unrighteous to forget" (Heb. 6:10) that will be diversely recognized and rewarded. He will distinguish degrees of faithful involvement in the fellowship of His work. There will be divine differentiation.

Nehemiah, having masterfully directed the rebuilding of the wall of Jerusalem, had a glimmering of this paradoxical truth. He could pray with devout sincerity, "Think upon me, my God, for good, according to all that I have done for this people," yet also report of the heathen "they perceived that this work was wrought of our God" (Neh. 5:19; 6:16). In the shared yoke, we pull together with

Christ, accepting His invitation to the fellowship of His sufferings and His work. We exert those powers with which He has endowed us, though less constantly and capably than He, and are graciously credited by Him for what we do.

If our part in the yoke-work is said to be consequential and rewardable by God, is it therefore appropriate for our own as well as others' recognition? Paul brings together the divine and human aspects when he modestly reminds the Corinthians of his labors among them as the founder of their church. "I am the least of the apostles, that am not meet to be called an apostle, because I persecuted the church of God. But by the grace of God I am what I am: and his grace which was bestowed upon me was not in vain; but I laboured more abundantly than they all: yet not I, but the grace of God which was with me" (1 Cor. 15:9–10). Paul speaks to the Colossian Christians of his ongoing effort to "present every man perfect in Christ Jesus"—an endeavor "whereunto I also labour, striving according to his working, which worketh in me mightily" (Col. 1:28–29). The apostle labored on his side, but then it was after all God laboring through him. Still since it was his labor too, it was not inappropriate to speak of it, enabled by God, as his own also and be pleased with it.

To the Galatians Paul wrote, "Let every man prove his own work, and then shall he have rejoicing in himself alone, and not in another" (Gal. 6:4). Paul qualifies his point soon after, insisting he will not glory in his accomplishments as his Galatian rivals have done in theirs. "God forbid that I should glory, save in the cross of our Lord Jesus Christ, by whom the world is crucified unto me, and I unto the world" (Gal. 6:14). Paul can feel pleasure in what God has enabled him to do without vaunting his part in it or reveling in its success. There is evidently a difference between being pleased with the success of an undertaking on the one hand—"having rejoicing" in a job accomplished—and luxuriating in self-congratulation. Paul is not above exclaiming, near the close of his life, with evident satisfaction, "I have fought a good fight, I have finished my course, I have kept the faith" (2 Tim. 4:7).

If success in the will of God is somehow both the work of God and the work of man, it follows that pleasant feelings are natural and legitimate when expressed, as was Paul's, in a context of grateful dependency. It would be a foolish parent who would censure his children's expressions of personal satisfaction at their completion of a long day's work or a challenging project, insisting that such feelings are not in order since the enabling was entirely God's. It would be strange not to praise a child for work well done, even if father or mother had had the main hand in it. We need not insist on somber spirits from a Cub Scout hiking party after a hard climb to the summit or urge our graduating seniors and their families to mute their exuberance on Commencement Day—though modesty in both instances can be in evidence as well. It would be a surly sanctimony indeed that would deny high spirits at the successful completion of a task assigned by the heavenly Father and be otherwise than elated by His "well done."

For the Lord Himself promises such a commendation for faithful discipleship at the final judging of His own. "Well done, good and faithful servant," says the ruler in the parable of the talents picturing the divine Judge (Matt. 25:23). "Then," writes Paul, "shall every man have praise of God" (1 Cor. 4:5). Surely there is no conflict between the human and the divine in the biblical account of personal accomplishment. Both come together in the invitation to a shared endeavor and in the promised praise of God.

21

SELF-ESTEEM

If we may take pleasure in what God has enabled us to be and do in union with Him, where are we left in the controversial matter of self-esteem? The "self-esteem movement" in secular psychology posited a favorable self-estimate as fundamental to emotional health. Though the notion has lost ground in professional circles (some criminal types have been shown to have exceptionally high self-esteem), its authority in contemporary culture can hardly be said to have waned. A person's "self-image" is still popularly regarded as critical to his life success.

What is wrong with this concept can be quickly identified and disposed of. When Paul feels constrained by his Corinthian detractors to show why, in their terms, he deserves their respect—to "become a fool in glorying" (2 Cor. 12:11)—he does so but shows his discomfort throughout. He reminds them repeatedly that his human credentials, which their immaturity is forcing him to display, are quite irrelevant to his apostolic claim on their obedience. He is momentarily adopting the self-promotional manner they admire in order to shame them. Make no mistake about it, says Paul, "He that glorieth, let him glory in the Lord" (2 Cor. 10:17), echoing Jeremiah 9:24.

Paul's stance on pride is everywhere apparent in his writings, no-where more than in the passage from Habakkuk so central in his theology: "Behold, his soul which is lifted up is not upright in him: but the just shall live by his faith" (2:4). Pride is of all mindsets the one that most directly challenges the rule of God. Even the prideful countenance is odious to Him (Ps. 18:27; Prov. 6:17). Followers of Christ are to "be clothed with humility: for God resisteth the proud, and giveth grace to the humble" (1 Pet. 5:5). The fundamental need of a disordered nature is not a boost in prideful self-esteem.

Yet we may combat the error of the "self-esteem" movement with-out losing its element of truth. A measured self-regard, as we have seen, is implied when Paul instructs his Christian reader "not to think of himself more highly than he ought to think; but to think soberly, according as God hath dealt to every man the measure of faith" (Rom. 12:3). In other words, he is not to value his worth above the common shared worth of other Christians. It is also implied when, with regard to competitive self-valuing, Paul tells the Philippians, "Let nothing be done through strife or vainglory; but in lowliness of mind let each esteem other better than them-selves" (2:3). Our estimation of others, in questions of preference, is to exceed our estimation of ourselves. The injunction does not require obsessive self-degradation. Paul told the Corinthians that God had provided him a safeguard against pride by giving him a "thorn in the flesh" lest he "should be exalted above measure" (2 Cor. 12:7). At that very moment in the epistle, Paul was arguing he was due their respect. Scripture is exact in moral definition.

Notice again that modest thinking about ourselves and generous thinking toward others in no way conflict with the truth of our importance as God's handiwork. The weakest of Christians is to be respected as a valued object of the Creator's attentive care and an instrument of His purpose. Paul, as we noted, assailed the proud

Roman Christians who, on the basis of their superior knowledge, trampled upon the simple scruples of some Jewish fellow believers. They were not, for the sake of food, to "destroy . . . the work of God" (Rom. 14:20).

It is a needed message for many a downcast saint that he is indeed, whatever his doubts, a cherished "work of God." Each redeemed life is too precious and too greatly privileged to languish in self-contempt. The Christian must never forget, on the one hand, his total dependency upon His Creator and, on the other, what he is and is destined for in the plan of God. The Almighty, observed the philosopher William James in an unaccountable flash of insight, "has larger thoughts about us than we have about ourselves."

How to keep this proper self-regard from slipping into a censurable self-esteem is a problem that has confronted believers in all ages and meets us every day. The enemy of our souls makes it his business to pervert good into evil, to transform the legitimate into sin. High spirits can all too easily slip into the "haughty spirit" that "goeth . . . before a fall" (Prov. 16:18). Our high spirits need not mutate into pride if we accept realistically and gratefully what we are and have in God. We can hardly be thankful for that which we credit to ourselves.

We can follow Paul's example. We can winnow down what we rejoice in about ourselves to the shared essentials of redeemed humanity. Jesus told the disciples, exhilarated from their power to cast out demons, to "rejoice not, that the spirits are subject unto you; but rather rejoice, because your names are written in heaven" (Luke 10:20). They no doubt were busy comparing exploits instead of delighting in their common status as workers with their Master and citizens of His kingdom. Paul, facing death, was buoyed by the sense that he had finished well the course of life given to him and that he had a reward waiting for him. "Henceforth there is laid up for me a crown of righteousness, which the Lord, the righteous judge, shall give me at that day." He then added modestly as if to deny his singularity in this respect, "And not to me only, but unto all them also that love his appearing" (2 Tim. 4:8).

The common stock of what we possess in Christ includes paradoxically the uniqueness about each of us. Every Christian is a separate work of God, particularly fashioned to reflect and serve his Lord in a special way. Each is endowed with an exquisitely blended set of gifts, elegantly bounded with limitations, so as to render him a gift to others—a special gift—and his life a returnable gift to God.

What are called handicaps can hedge us in to success in paths of greatest blessing. Because of her blindness Fanny Crosby could do little but write poetry, including some of our best-loved hymns. Because a vocal impairment took him out of the pulpit in his early fifties, a pastor in a small Southern town had to content himself largely with writing little gems for his community newspaper that would reach his entire town. Because of a heart condition in youth that kept him in bed for a year and physically restricted him thereafter, a former colleague of mine became fascinated with Scripture. He began a detailed study of the Bible that would last a lifetime, affecting thousands who would sit in his classes, hear his preaching, and read his books.

Natural deficits are as important as natural assets in the service of God. Now more than ever the world can be reached from a wheelchair and influenced for God. We may justly take pleasure in the sum of what we are, not omitting to remember "it is he that hath made us, and not we ourselves" (Ps. 100:3) and that He Who has made us has also made our richly endowed brethren in Christ.

Sinful self-esteem is the estimation of one's gifts and achievements to the advantage of oneself over others. The Pharisee condemned in Jesus' parable prayed, "God, I thank thee that I am not as other men are" (Luke 18:11). Paul severely warns against competitive self-valuing. "We dare not make ourselves of the number, or compare ourselves with some others that commend themselves . . . by themselves," to which he adds, "they measuring themselves by themselves, and comparing themselves among themselves, are not wise" (2 Cor. 10:12). The apostle engaged in self-exaltation only ironically and in order to condemn it. He would boast only of his "infirmities"—the deficiencies in spite of which God had helped him succeed (2 Cor. 12:9) and had gotten glory to Himself. But he did not belittle the importance of his efforts for God, and the measure of his joy when God enabled them to succeed was the measure of his grief when they failed.

22

GRATIFICATION

High spirits arise from the gratification of desires, of trivial wishes as well as deep yearnings. They can come from recognizable causes but can come also unaccountably, from no evident source, refreshing us as a sudden cool breeze soothes a field worker on a sultry summer afternoon. Though only momentary, these fleeting visits come purposefully, revitalizing us and reminding us of the goodness of God. Whether from identifiable causes or from mysterious fluctuations of the psyche, high spirits restore to our mental landscape the large picture of God's activity in our personal world, supplying a blessed context to our sorrows and struggles. Our "high places" are lookouts on our life paths affording inspirational clarifying vistas unavailable from the valley or the low plain. Such moments are gifts from God. They are to be received gratefully and made use of for His praise and in His service. They comfort our thoughts with the realization that we indeed matter to God.

There is practical value in this insight. Since we matter to God, we may matter to ourselves—a fact, when recognized, that facilitates self-surrender. To be grateful for God's investment in my life, His personal interest in it, His costly involvement in it, His fashioning of it for His good and mine, for His pleasure and mine, is as noted earlier a giant stride toward true humility and spiritual submission. When a child of God is able to see his own good and God's as one and the same, he can surrender all the more easily to the will of God, knowing that there is no real loss in personal surrender. The bride in the Song of Solomon cares about herself. She has a sense of her own dignity and worth that makes all the more meaningful her yielding to her lover.

This sense of personal worth then is not the carnal self-centeredness we have in mind when we condemn pride under the name of self-esteem. God-centeredness raises all our relationships, including our relation to ourselves—to our sense of our true purposes, values, happiness, and ultimate good. Our sense of our value comes from what God has invested in us and desires for us and desires for Himself in us, not from what we are on our own account. Our sense of the value of our lives comes from God's gracious invitation to live in fellowship with Him and, with His help, to accomplish much for Him. It does not come from thoughts of superiority to others.

A Christian is gratified by that for which he is grateful. Of all the things he should fear in his life, the greatest is that as life goes on he should forget to be grateful. Ingratitude, wrote Shakespeare, is "as the serpent's tooth." It poisons like nothing else a relationship between parent and child, between friend and friend, and between man and his Maker. In the lowest circle of Dante's hell were the extreme ingrates—the betrayers of benefactors. Ingratitude has been thought to be the most detestable of sins.

It may also be the most impoverishing. There is nothing that sweetens a life like gratitude—a recognition of benefits accruing from another's bounty. Among these benefits for which we are grateful is not what the Pharisee gave thanks for in his prayer, that he was not like other men. We are grateful rather for the good things all Christians possess together: God's crafting and provisioning of their lives and His welcome to fellowship and service. The true Christian is thankful he *is* like other men, those that know God, in what he has been given in salvation and in ongoing blessings. Included in what he has been given are opportunities to serve his divine benefactor in ways He promises to recognize and reward.

Here we see the importance to our gratitude of understanding the worth of the self. When we surrender ourselves to God, we yield something of value so it can become more valuable—more valuable to God, which is the greater truth, but also more valuable to ourselves. If to give is more blessed than to receive, to offer a valuable gift is more blessed than to give a poor one. When we offer God ourselves, the greatest gift of which we are capable, and are assured, as we may be, of its gracious acceptance, we have true gratification, and our spirits may indeed justly soar.

THE SUFFERING SELF

I am a woman of a sorrowful spirit . . . but have poured
out my soul before the Lord.

1 Samuel 1:15

23

FROM THE DEPTHS

Our spirits do not always soar, as we well know. In fact, they may sink more often than they soar. It is time then to make the same claim for low spirits made for high—that they are no less warranted by Scripture and can work for good. We shall see that low spirits are no surer indications of spiritual failure than are high spirits of spiritual success. Indeed, our emotional lows can be divinely purposed and productive.

Let us be clear from the start that low spirits, like all pain, are ultimately rooted in sin. All human beings have suffered the effects of Adam's sin, even those "that had not sinned after the similitude of Adam's transgression" (Rom. 5:14). The Savior Himself, though sinless, was not exempt from these effects. We know from the Gospel record that He could experience physical fatigue (John 4:6). We also know He could suffer emotional agitation and heaviness (Mark 14:33). Obviously He endured physical and emotional pain from causes for which He was not responsible. He was "in all points tempted like as we are, yet without sin" (Heb. 4:15).

Jesus' followers, like their Master, have suffered both physical and mental affliction because of their identification with

Him—"trial of cruel mockings and scourgings"—though on an infinitely lesser scale (Heb. 11:36). Peter writes to persecuted believers who "are in heaviness through manifold temptations" yet who still are able to "rejoice with joy unspeakable and full of glory" (1 Pet. 1:6, 8). Paul speaks of being "sorrowful, yet alway rejoicing" (2 Cor. 6:10).

To hold that low spirits can exist guiltlessly is not of course to deny that we can have a great deal to do with the occurrence and recurrence of our troubles. If we are honest with ourselves, we know that much of what we endure emotionally we bring upon ourselves. It is also not to deny that there is enough sinfulness in each of us to justify far more trouble and pain than could be packed into a lifetime. Creatures who deserve hell deserve lesser pains as well. Yet the Savior made it clear there is no necessary relation between personal distress and personal behavior (John 9:2–3). One can suffer simply because he lives in a fallen world.

Scripture abounds in instances of innocent mental suffering. Jesus, we have seen, warned His disciples of a coming interval of sadness when He would be gone from them. "Verily, verily, I say unto you, That ye shall weep and lament, but the world shall rejoice: and ye shall be sorrowful, but your sorrow shall be turned into joy. . . . And ye now therefore have sorrow: but I will see you again, and your heart shall rejoice, and your joy no man taketh from you" (John 16:20, 22). He did not reprimand them for sorrowing or warn them against dejection, but gave them a promise to mitigate their sorrow, telling them it would end in joy.

Paul speaks of his mental distress upon entering Macedonia, when "without were fightings" and "within were fears," and of having been relieved by refreshing news from a coworker. "God, that comforteth those that are cast down, comforted us by the coming of Titus" (2 Cor. 7:5–6). Later Paul tells of his gratitude to God for sparing the life of his ill "brother and companion in labour" Epaphroditus, "lest I should have sorrow upon sorrow" (Phil. 2:25, 27). The apostle, like his Master, was "a man of sorrows, and acquainted with grief" (Isa.53:3).

The Psalms present emotional down times of some severity and continuance. Psalm 93 shows the inspired poet encouraging himself in the Lord. Though "the floods have lifted up their voice," yet "the Lord on high is mightier than the noise of many waters, yea, than the mighty waves of the sea" (93:3–4). The psalmist has learned, as would later the twelve disciples, that his Lord is master of waves and wind—that, in the words of David, "the Lord sitteth upon the flood" (Ps. 29:10). The truth of divine omnipotence is well established in his mind, and he relies on it in times of distress.

Yet from the Psalms we learn also that the calming of the storm does not always follow immediately the prayer for the calming. In section 4 of the "long Psalm," the prayer begins, "My soul cleaveth unto the dust: quicken thou me according to thy word," and continues, "My soul melteth for heaviness: strengthen thou me according unto thy word." There may be some space in time as there is in the text before mental energies are restored. "I will run the way of thy commandments, when thou shalt enlarge my heart" (119:25, 28, 32). The inspired petitioner is firm of purpose ("I have chosen the way of truth," v. 30) and of commitment ("I have stuck unto thy testimonies," v. 31), but the full performance of his purpose and commitment awaits the Lord's calming of the storm in his mind.

In a pair of psalms, 42 and 43, David feels isolated from God and yearns for a sense of His presence. "As the hart panteth after the water brooks, so panteth my soul after thee, O God. . . . My tears have been my meat day and night, while they continually say unto me, Where is thy God?" (42:1, 3). He admonishes himself: "Why art thou cast down, O my soul? and why art thou disquieted in me? hope thou in God: for I shall yet praise him for the help of his countenance" (v. 5). He renews his plea: "O my God, my soul is cast down within me . . . all thy waves and thy billows are gone over me" (vv. 6–7). He again admonishes himself, "Why art thou cast down, O my soul? and why art thou disquieted within me? hope thou in God: for I shall yet praise him, who is the health of my countenance, and my God" (v. 11). David is in acute mental distress because of threatening circumstances and pours out his heart to God. His spirit is dejected ("cast down") and turbulent ("disquieted"). He feels shut off from fellowship with his Maker.

Psalm 43, a sequel to 42, expresses similar distress ("why dost thou cast me off?" v. 2) and ends similarly in hopeful purpose: "I shall yet praise him . . ." (v. 5). The recurring sequence of prayer and self-encouragement in these two psalms suggests that the mental distress was of some duration and had yet to be relieved at the close of the second one. David's faith appears in his trust that his emotional suffering will eventually end: "I shall yet praise him," he declares in faith, though at the moment his faith has yet to be realized.

If David composed Psalms 42 and 43 in flight from his son Absalom, we may reasonably suspect that physical fatigue had something to do with his state of mind. It seems also more than likely that physical exhaustion had something to do with the depression of Elijah under the juniper tree desiring God to take his life. The angel of the Lord did not censure him for his emotional state but caused him to sleep, provided him food and drink, and put him in mind of his purpose. "Arise and eat; because the journey is too great for thee" (1 Kings 19:7). From the shadow of the juniper tree, Elijah traveled to Mount Sinai for an encounter with God like that of Moses centuries before. He found a cave and "lodged there" (v. 9). Here however spiritual issues came into play. Life as a cave-dwelling hermit was evidently not what God had intended for Elijah, for his behavior incurred a rebuke: "What doest thou here, Elijah?" (v. 9). His depression was taking the direction of morbid withdrawal and required spiritual correction. Still Elijah again was given sustenance and something to do. As the causes of his depression were both natural and spiritual, so also were the therapies.

There is nothing especially modern about the idea that human beings are put together in such a way that the mind affects the body and the body the mind. The French philosopher Rene Descartes declared as a truism that the mind not only thinks but also "can act and suffer along with the body."[1] The eminent evangelical surgeon-pathologist John Cheyne, in *Essays on Partial Derangement of the Mind*,[2] concludes from his success treating asylum inmates and lesser cases that emotional disorders are due usually to physical rather than moral causes. Cheyne's view concurs with today's medical knowledge and common observation that physical trauma—serious surgery or stroke, for example—and chemical imbalance can bring on depression.

The reverse is also true. It has long been known that mind states can affect the body. "A merry heart doeth good like a medicine: but a broken spirit drieth the bones" (Prov. 17:22). It is no recent discovery that a patient's mental attitude can speed or slow the healing process. We learn from Scripture that acute mental stress can be physically disabling. Daniel's vision of the ram and the goat and Gabriel's interpretation of it put the prophet in momentary shock and left him too weakened to work. "And I Daniel fainted, and was sick certain days; afterward I rose up, and did the king's business" (Dan. 8:27). Scripture supports today's medical consensus on the interinvolvement of body and mind.

Low spirits then can be a natural response to physical disorders. They can also come from causes entirely mental. Daniel speaks repeatedly of his spirit being "troubled" by his dreams. Their mental causes are diverse. They may arise as in Ahab from guilt or frustration (1 Kings 20:43; 21:4), or as in Saul from fear or anger or wounded pride (1 Sam. 18:10). They may accompany a penitent spirit, grief for a loved one lost to the next world or (more crushingly) to the present one. They may be punitive as they were for Saul (1 Sam. 18:10) or constructive as for Job. They may be also, as in Job's case, due to satanic attack. They may be part of the mind's recuperation, for emotional exhaustion can follow emotional exertion in a restorative way. Modern medicine has learned that an artificially induced coma following extreme trauma can help the healing process. Whether innocent or not in their immediate cause, these downward moods are capable of good: to indicate defective character and behavior, to dampen appetites, to strip a life of triviality and center it usefully, to restore spent energies and bring about goodly change.

The positive uses of low spirits go beyond simply getting problem areas corrected. Exceptionally creative persons often remark that productive surges come between troughs of troubled dullness. Richard Restak, professor of neurology and author of ten books on the brain, suspects a link between emotional lows and creativity, observing that "writers have a high prevalence of depression and bipolar disorder (manic-depression)." Mood disorders, he remarks, seem to be more common among especially creative people.[3]

The emotional downturns noted by Restak are not limited to gifted artists. Even a school child, assigned a paper or project requiring sustained creative effort, may suffer through a period of frustrating inertia before getting underway. He pokes around in the library, shuffles and reshuffles his notes, doodles, stares into space, repeats the cycle, all the while in an anxious dullness of spirit that tests his resolve. At last from what has seemed a bottomless, endless muddle emerges a discernible shape—cosmos from chaos.

Perhaps this troubled process simply comes with life in a fallen world. In sorrow, the young problem solver conceives his idea, and with the sweat of his brain labors to bring it into existence. But the pain of the process, physical and emotional, is not itself blameworthy, and the process can be blessed of God.

Still what most claims our attention in this investigation are those intermittent seemingly uncaused spells of low spirits that affect almost everyone for no discernible reason. Whether short or long, mild or severe, provoked or not by surroundings, they come to us as surely as they do unpredictably. The lows and highs can seem necessary to each other. Has anyone not noticed how the down times can leave in their wake fresh energies and brighter, broader vistas and how the dizzy raptures of the heights are profitably tempered by the downward critical turn in the cycle? No pain need be wasted in the economy of God.

I am convinced that this ebb and flow of the spirits—our "depths" and our "high places"—is a universal benign feature of human life. My observation tells me that the depths have a mysterious purgative and recuperative, even generative, function as they do in the life cycle of plants. It is characteristic of human life, observed Kierkegaard, that feasting begins in the evening, not at dawn.

24

THE DEEPER DEPTHS

For some, the coming of emotional lows is anticipated with a dread known only to them. Chronic sufferers from acute depression can become convinced they exist in a prison of pain and confusion that no one else can understand or will even try to understand. Adding to their distress is what they often hear from steadier souls who have learned very well how to master their Monday blues and are ready with advice on the subject. A strengthened will power, a raised sense of purpose and worth, a renewed awareness of all that is positive in life—these, they are told, will dissipate the gloom.

A Christian given to recurring bouts of depression who has been assured he would conquer it were he only to make fuller use of his spiritual resources has even more guilt to deal with. His problem, thus defined, is not just a shirking of personal responsibility; it is spiritual failure. He is failing to draw upon the help of God to deal with a problem in spiritual character. By allowing himself to remain depressed, he is disobedient—sinning not only against himself, his family, and others about him, but also and ultimately against an all-enabling God. His depression is morbid self-indulgence, a state of mind he could throw off were he to avail himself of God's power. There is no excuse for his inaction. The solution is simple: a renewed spiritual resolve and a change of heart.

So he is told. With well-intended matter-of-factness, low spirits of the most terrifying, disabling sort are bundled together with ordinary moodiness as obstinate, corrigible self-indulgence. As the sufferer takes the admonition to heart, his spirits sink toward despair. A moral failing has become also a spiritual failing. He feels estranged from fellow Christians and from God.

It is certainly true that depression can be rooted in mind states needing spiritual correction and that deliverance from such depression can be instantaneous. Sin-based attitudes such as envy and bitterness respond dramatically to spiritual correction. Emotional relief comes quickly when the cause of depression is a sin on the conscience. Confession, reparation, and heart surrender flood the mind with the peace promised by the Lord to His disciples (John 14:27). With such cases, spiritual counsel alone proves sufficient for the purpose.

But to assume that all low spirits are directly sin-related and indicative of spiritual failure does not follow. We know that physical illness and injury can bring periods of very low spirits. Stroke victims can experience severe depression, as can amputees. Painful, degenerative diseases can weaken the spirit and bring despondency. Depression can come to women from menopausal or postpartum irregularities, hypothyroidism, or other hormonal imbalance. To assume that guilt is the cause of these can be devastating to the afflicted person who cannot, try as he may, link his low spirits with an attitude or behavior for which he should be blamed. Like the chronic migraine sufferer, he lives in shadows even during the sunny intervals he knows from long experience will be followed by dark descents. During the down times he must use what means he has and hold steady until the darkness lifts.

Among his means are the spiritual and the practical. The eminent pastor-preacher Charles Spurgeon dealt with his recurring bouts of depression by preaching on themes of praise. William Cowper held off despair during savage emotional lows by writing poetry, including some of our most treasured hymns. The aged, blind poet John Milton, afflicted with gout, fought gloom by singing psalms and applying himself to his writing.

Spiritual counseling is of undeniable value here when it is rendered with judgment and tact. The virtues of patience and trust may need to be stressed to the ill or injured. Heeding medical instruction is an obedience issue. Keeping up the spiritual life and resting in the promises of God are always important reminders. But sensitivity is in order. Exhortations to cheerfulness are not always to the purpose. "As he that taketh away a garment in cold weather, and as vinegar upon nitre, so is he that singeth songs to a heavy heart" (Prov. 25:20). Nor are blanket condemnations. To be told that he, being a sinner by nature, deserves worse (though true for us all) is of little help to a sufferer. The deeper depths need not become deeper than they are.

We must tell chronic sufferers that what they contend with is an infirmity, not a sin—or not inevitably such—and that the God of all comfort has a feeling for His creatures' infirmities. He has experienced them Himself (Heb. 4:15). The God of ancient Israel understood heaviness of spirit. "I am pressed under you," He said, "as a cart is pressed that is full of sheaves" (Amos 2:13). He did not languish under His burden but continued His efforts to turn His people from their ruin, "rising early" under the load "and sending" His prophets to warn them (Jer. 25:4). His emotional suffering was both chronic and intense, recurring as well as severe. He was innocent of its cause.

The truth that suffering can be innocent and also purposive is a master theme of Scripture. It includes emotional as well as physical distress. During the era of the patriarchs or not long after in a region east of the Jordan River, God delivered to Satan for testing a man of proven character and let him undergo the loss of almost everything meaningful to him on earth except his life. He did so for our benefit as well as his. "Hast thou considered my servant Job?" said God to Satan (1:8), presenting him also for our consideration.

At stake was Job's integrity. Would Satan be able to shake his faith in God and in God's blessings on his life? Job allowed that he was like all other men a sinner but continued insisting he had lived a blameless life, sincere and wholehearted in his devotion to God and his treatment of others. He knew he was no hypocrite and rejected the charges leveled against him by his accusers. Their condemnation of him was unjust, wrong in its factual particulars and wrong in its premise that suffering is necessarily due to sin. But still Job was confused. It seemed God had withdrawn His face but not His hand. "Oh that I knew where I might find him! . . . I go forward, but he is not there; and backward, but I cannot perceive him: on the left hand, where he doth work, but I cannot behold him: he hideth himself on the right hand, that I cannot see him" (23:3, 8–9). Yet Job retained his faith in divine purpose. "He knoweth the way that I take," and "when he hath tried me, I shall come forth as gold" (23:10).

When God took over the examination of Job, the focus shifted from Job's past life to Job's understanding of God. Job had come to think of God as an adversary and wished to make his case to Him in open court. The divine Judge took Job, as it were, into His chambers and vindicated Himself. He revealed His perfect knowledge of the minutest features of His world as well as those vastly beyond Job's comprehension, proving that nothing about

Job's suffering could have escaped Him. He knows and rules all in wisdom and goodness.

The argument is what logicians call *a fortiori*: if A, how much more B? If the God of the universe knows the intricacies of weather patterns, He will surely know the eddying currents of a human life. If He keeps the stars in place, He will preside over the difficulties of His human creatures. If He cares about a wild donkey and a vulture, He will care about a Job. If He is present when the wild goats give birth, He will be at hand during human sorrow and anguish. Job is stricken with shame for having doubted the goodness and greatness of his God while cheered by the assurance God is never less present when He hides himself than when He announces His presence from a whirlwind.

After vindicating Himself to Job, God vindicated Job to Job's three friends. They "have not spoken of me the thing that is right, as my servant Job hath." God had been there all the time, listening to what was being said, cruelly by Job's antagonists and sincerely if not always temperately by Job. Only after expensive sacrifices and Job's intercession would the friends escape being dealt with severely "after [their] folly" as God deals with false accusers of the good (42:8). Their folly exceeded the foolishness of the godly tormented man, who allowed some words to escape him that he later greatly rued. Job's friends were made to understand that it was they, not Job, who lacked righteous standing with God and that God in fact treasured Job's righteous character and sincere heart. These heartless theoreticians were faced with the falseness and malice of their own premises.

Job's sudden steep descent was not due to his sin. His life pattern was broken by conditions over which he had no control. Satan directed his torments, attacking him totally. His comforters became his antagonists, subjecting him to a theological battering that linked all deprivations with sin. In Job's testing God has given us an instance in which it was cruelly inappropriate to attribute sin to a man in a dejected condition, suffering in body and even more in mind. God took over the counseling session and targeted the real need of the counselee, not once rebuking him for his depressed mind state. He countered Job's sense of rejection by disclosing in person the greatness and goodness of Himself.

Few if any have sounded deeper depths and descended into them more precipitously than did Job. Few have experienced more painfully in these depths the seeming absence of God and suffered more in body and mind than he. And few have drawn more good from their sufferings than did Job. And so, all who suffer in the deeper depths would do well to consider not only what Job lost during his misery but also what he gained. We are told he regained family and friends and enormous wealth, but that was not the whole of it or even the most important part. And here we come to the special opportunity of all who suffer in the deeper depths.

The suffering of Job raised his relationship with God. From his anguish came a friendship with God requiring yet transcending mere obedience. To be a friend, said the Lord, is a vastly higher station than to be a servant, "for the servant knoweth not what his lord doeth" (John 15:15). God shared with Job things Job did not know, such things as He may have shared with Adam in the garden. In the process God drew Job into a new intimacy with Himself, revealing Himself personally as the Friend Job had not known.

25

THE LONG GRIEF

The severest challenge to the spirits may be not the occasional or recurring deep descents in the emotional life but a continuing low. A loss comes that is keen and enduring, shadowing the life for years, perhaps to its end. It may raise doubt about life's purpose and, for the Christian, questions about God's promises of peace and joy.

The loss may be the death of a loved one, and with it a huge chunk of a life that was shared. Jacob, after being shown the torn robe of his son Joseph, grieved "many days," refusing to put off his mourning clothes. "I will go down into the grave unto my son mourning," he said (Gen. 37:34–35). The loss may be what can seem even more consequential and be felt even worse, the loss of a child to sin and the world. "A foolish son is the heaviness of his mother," observes the wise man of Proverbs, speaking of an unshakable weight, oppressing the heart and weakening the spirit (10:1). Scripture places much of the burden of family harmony on the obedience of children, who may little realize the extent to which they affect the emotional health of their parents (10:1). Concerning her son Esau's choice of wives in defiance of his parents, Rebekah exclaimed, "I am weary of my life because of these daughters of Heth" (Gen. 27:46). She saw no end to her misery from the ruinous decision of her son.

Paul knew the weight of an ongoing dispiriting grief. He speaks of the "great heaviness and continual sorrow" pressing on him from the unbelief of his people, the Jews. He could wish himself "accursed from Christ" if it would secure their salvation (Rom. 9:2–3). His burdens were with him at the end of his life. Demas, a son in the faith, had forsaken him for "this present world" (2 Tim. 4:10). His ministry had been repudiated by the churches of Galatia, the area of his first missionary endeavor.

Such a grief may be an impairment from birth. It may be a lifelong disfiguring injury. It may be a crushing blow to a prosperous financial future or to the reputation. It may be the loss of a treasured skill. It may be the bedside duty of caring for a loved one who is sinking irreversibly over time, for whom sorrowing has already begun and care can exhaust beyond imagination. For some it is a childless marriage, for others a marriage crippled by a spouse's sin, for still others no marriage at all.

To all who outlive their youth will come that long descent in physical strength and appearance, which Scripture reminds us to expect. "He hath made every thing beautiful in his time" says the wise man, but its time is not always (Eccles. 3:11). "We all do fade as a leaf," writes the prophet Isaiah, the loss of color portending the fall to the ground (Isa. 64:6). "Let the beauty of the Lord . . . be upon us," urges the aging Moses (Ps. 90:17), speaking of a beauty more to be sought than the physical, and yet nature's beauty is also His beauty. There is something justly lamentable in what is lost to the years as beauty and strength diminish with the passing of time.

To feel sorrow from the loss of something valued is natural to our existence in a fallen world. We have from our Creator pressing desires to live, to grow, to acquire and achieve and enjoy. We love, and we yearn to have our love returned. These desires are always subject to frustration. When they are thwarted, we are rightly sad if our sadness is scaled to the value of the object that was lost and to the permanency of the loss. Our sadness speaks of our respect for what we have lost; and this respect, if commensurate with its true value, is entirely natural and legitimate. But a sense of loss can settle in and become more than it should be. A feeling of deprivation can become a conviction of desolation and take over a life. That it need not do so, even in the extremest of sorrows, we may be assured from examples in Scripture.

Joseph suffered mental anguish during his early years in Egypt. Sold into slavery by his brothers and betrayed by his master's wife, he entered prison at eighteen, having lost his family. At thirty he left prison, having lost his youth. He endured long years of sadness of the kind that can shatter the spirit and wither the will. His inner pain, undiminished after ten years of confinement, appears in his urgent plea to the butler. "But think on me when it shall be well with thee, and shew kindness, I pray thee, unto me, and make mention of me unto Pharaoh, and bring me out of this house" (Gen. 40:14). Psalm 105 speaks poignantly of the young Joseph when it tells us that his "feet they hurt with fetters" and "he was laid in iron" (105:18). The original Hebrew tells us that his "soul was laid in iron." His affliction was not only physical. It attacked his spirit.

An additional two years would pass before Joseph was released, during which time he had no human reason to think he would ever escape his confinement. Later, his grief and his resiliency of spirit would appear in his names for his children. He named the elder Manasseh, "making to forget"; "for God, said he, hath made me forget all my toil, and all my father's house." He named the younger Ephraim, "fruitfulness"; "for God hath caused me to be fruitful in the land of my affliction" (Gen. 41:51–52). Forgetting and fruitfulness were works of grace in Joseph during and beyond the long dark years of his incarceration. "They that sow in tears shall reap in joy" is the promise of Scripture, borne out in this remarkable life (Ps. 126:5).

Joseph knew the full measure of soul-wrenching sadness, but he seems not to have fallen to despair. His words to the butler and baker and later to Pharaoh indicate he had remained in touch with his father's God. He had found in the dimness of his long trial what the three Hebrew youths in Daniel would discover in the white heat of their testing: a divine Companion and Friend.

For Joseph, like Job, was being schooled by mental distress in the goodness and wisdom of God. His affliction must have seemed to him as total and final as Job's. It was of greater duration. But from it was to emerge a life as beautiful as any in Scripture apart from the Savior's, an example of obedient faith to be thrown up to Satan's cynicism as confidently as was Job's. Interpreters differ on whether, or the extent to which, the character and life of Joseph in the Old Testament are intended to prefigure the person and mission of Christ in the New. Joseph is not named in Scripture as a type of Christ. Perhaps the point of the parallel is that protracted misery once fashioned a person so very like what we see of God in our Savior that the similarities between him and the Lord are unmistakable. In Joseph the long grief had done its good work.

The best we may expect in this world is the joy of our Lord—a mingled joy, shadowed by disappointment yet alive with confidence in His promises and the comfort of His presence. Isaiah speaks literally of the transformation of the desert during the reign of Messiah, when it "shall rejoice, and blossom as the rose" (35:1). He also speaks metaphorically of the transformation of the character of the people, who will be "like a watered garden, and like a spring of water, whose waters fail not" (58:11). The image is frequent in Scripture. Though our lives may seem poor in outward circumstances, a veritable drought of earthly possibilities, they need not exhibit features of that famine described by Amos, one not "of bread, nor a thirst for water, but of hearing the words of the Lord" (8:11). In low deserts can be found oases and aquifers fed by what in the descending gorges are only streams.

For there can be different kinds of valleys. So observed the scholar-pastor Handley Moule, commenting on 1 Kings 20. "Life sinks into a dark pass sometimes, in great anxieties, or bitter disappointments." On the other hand, life can appear "not so much like a deep valley as like a broad, open plain, hot and featureless, where the land is flat and the air is faint." God's authority, remarks Moule, extends not just to the "deeper depths" but also to those long sun-scorched stretches with endlessly receding horizons that can draw down the spirit over time. "Master, carest thou not that we perish?" we may cry with the disciples of old (Mark 4:38). God is "jealous for His glory" in both valleys of the spirit, but it is the second kind—the long grief—that for many Christians will call forth the greatest exertions of faith.[1]

Luke's account of the Savior's birth tells of a woman, frequenting the temple, who had been widowed in the seventh year of her marriage, eighty-four years before. Rather than languishing in her long grief, she "served God with fastings and prayers night and day" (2:37). She found in her dire human necessity a divine opportunity. Her consecrated service in simple ways available to her was not overlooked by the God to Whom she had given her life. Her encounter with the Christ child found a place in the birth narrative of Luke's Gospel. Her long grief was crowned by a moment of singular honor and extraordinary joy.

26

THE SORROW OF THE WORLD

Would that the long grief always ended in the exuberance of the aged prophetess of Luke's narrative. Still her life would have been a triumph even had it not concluded the way it did. During her long widowhood Anna had been busy ministering in prayer and praise rather than waiting fretfully for her life to take a better turn and sinking into despondency when it did not. There was something about her that kept her from bitter, apathetic dejection. The old Greeks and Romans would have said she had mastered her feelings. We would say she was managing them productively. We can be certain she was doing so not by sheer strength of will and self-discipline, those prideful virtues of the early philosophers, but through her faith in God. Her spirits were buoyed by the peace and joy that go with obedient trust.

Sadly, a long grief such as Anna's can settle into lethargic despair. In the old scheme of the seven deadly sins, the sin of sloth was conjoined with despair. There is moral insight in the linkage. Lethargy can produce failure in life, and failure can bring despair, a paralyzing conviction of hopelessness. The wise man of Proverbs shows the dismal effect of sloth in a scene guaranteed to yield despair. "I went by the field of the slothful, and by the vine-yard of the man void of understanding; and, lo, it was all grown over with thorns, and nettles had covered the face thereof" (Prov. 24:30–31). Lethargy in turn is reinforced by despair, the cycle spiraling down to a cessation of the effort and even the desire to amend. The end-state of despair is a refusal of hope and the death of the will.

For this reason despair was thought to be the most conclusively deadly of the deadly sins. It amounted to a giving up on life. Spiritually the victim gives up on God's grace, determined to seek it no more, to remain in remorse rather than pursue hope through repentance. The ultimate act of despair was the taking of one's life. Spiritual suicide could occur before death, a prelim-inary state in which the soul dismisses its hope, refuses further opportunity, and is reconciled to its own ruin. The soul is dead before the body reaches the grave.

That a person could act so irrationally against his own good is strange indeed, but there is biblical support for the notion. We can hear the appeal of God to the despairing Jewish exiles through His prophet Ezekiel: "If our transgressions and our sins be upon us, and we pine away in them, how should we then live? . . . As I live, saith the Lord God, I have no pleasure in the death of the wicked; but that the wicked turn from his way and live: turn ye, turn ye from your evil ways; for why will ye die, O house of Israel?" (33:10–11).

God tells Jeremiah, prophesying before the exile, that He desires to bless His people but is about to "repent of the good, where-with . . . I would benefit them." He urges a change of heart and behavior: "Return ye now every one from his evil way, and make your ways and your doings good." His hearers respond in a way that reads like a spiritual death wish. "There is no hope: but we will walk after our own devices, and we will every one do the imagination of his evil heart" (Jer. 18:10–12). We will strut to our destruction, and let that be the end of the matter.

It is evident that an awareness of guilt does not inevitably soften a sinner's heart. The contrary is all too often the case. His heart can harden toward God's invitation, toward the very means of his deliverance. The committed sinner prefers his dangerous condition to its remedy, assuring himself there is no hope and therefore no reason to trouble himself about it. If he cares about himself at all, he lives in defiant remorse. Paul contrasts the "godly sorrow" that "worketh repentance to salvation" with "the sorrow of the world" that "worketh death" (2 Cor. 7:10).

Despair was thought in former times to derive not only from inactivity but also from misperception. It could result from false values. "Ye have taken away my gods which I made . . . and what have I more?" says Micah the Ephraimite after the Danites have plundered his household shrine (Judg. 18:24). Micah's home deities had not protected him, and yet he lamented the loss of them all the same. There is a stubbornness here—a refusal to recognize the foolish basis of his life.

Despair could result from confused values. A genuine earthly good can be granted a higher status than it warrants so that the loss of it is like the loss of Micah's idols. A person continues to grieve over a legitimate loss but not to any good purpose. What was at first natural and understandable in sadness transmutes into obstinate melancholy. The grieving soul sinks no less surely than were the cause of its despondency less substantial than it is. An authority on the traditional vices observes of despair that "one commits it by yielding . . . to worldly disappointments as if they mattered supremely."[1] Locked in a deadly embrace with failed values, the despondent victim dooms himself before he reaches the grave. Whether from resistance to God or from disappointment in life, the sin of despair, the "sorrow of the world," is a deadly spell.

27

DESPAIR AND PRIDE

In this older thought, despair is linked with pride as one of the two great counterpoised threats to the soul. The attacks of pride and despair coordinate with the rise and fall of the emotions, defeating their victim at his most vulnerable times. This insight concurs with what we know of our great adversary. Satan takes advantage of what are at first innocent emotional states. He practices upon the immaturity of his victims. They have not learned how to enjoy success and endure disappointment without falling into their associated temptations. They have yet to learn, in Paul's phrase, "both how to be abased" and "how to abound" (Phil. 4:12).

In the converted, pride and despair defeat faith and hope, virtues sustaining the spiritual life. In the unconverted, pride and despair drive unbelief. Pride is the active, despair the passive, rejection of God. They typically occur in locked sequence. Prideful imaginings and undertakings carry a certain unrealism with them, which when tested by harsh circumstance can bring mortifying disappointment, yielding bitter, arrogant despair. Countless life narratives have followed this plot line. The story is as old as man.

The divine invitation of salvation by grace through faith in Jesus Christ is a direct challenge to these sinful mind states. Rejections of the gospel generally divide along the lines of pride and despair. The content of the "good news" explains why that is so. Let us recall where it begins in the New Testament. "Unto you is born this day in the city of David a Saviour, which is Christ the Lord," announced the heavenly multitude to the amazed shepherds in Luke 2:11. This One to be born, the angel Gabriel had said to Joseph in a dream, would "save his people from their sins" (Matt. 1:21). What was needed of His people and of all people was salvation from sin. It was a gift by the Great King to men of good will in expectation of their repentance and acceptance of His rule. It promised freedom from sin's power and from eternal punishment, a freedom conditioned on belief in the One Who would sacrifice Himself to make it possible. The offer, first extended to Israel, would be given to all mankind.

The good news for the shepherds is our good news also. It is a welcome but also a warning, carrying grave consequences for those who reject it. Why, one might wonder, would anyone reject it? The reasons may seem strange. For some the invitation is too simple and the requirement too easy to be taken seriously. It is too demeaning. It clashes with pride. Paul makes very clear that the gospel allows no room for self-validation. "By grace are ye saved through faith; and that not of yourselves: it is the gift of God: not of works, lest any man should boast" (Eph. 2:8–9).

For others just the opposite is the case. The good news is too demanding. It reaches too far into the life. It raises too high its standard of discipleship. It engenders despair. "I will follow thee whithersoever thou goest," said a scribe, who however seems to have reconsidered after Jesus' reply: "The foxes have holes, and the birds of the air have nests; but the Son of man hath not where to lay his head" (Matt. 8:19–20).

The cost of acceptance was too steep for a rich young man of sincere intention who came to Jesus to settle the issue of his soul's future. He came running and kneeled at Jesus' feet and earnestly asked, "What shall I do to inherit eternal life?" He got the whole matter wrong, of course, with his prideful assumption that eternal life was a commodity to be purchased by good works. Jesus welcomed him but gave him something to do that touched him at the tender point of his life values. "Sell all that thou hast, and distribute unto the poor, and thou shall have treasure in heaven: and come, follow me." This answer staggered the young man and left him dismayed. "When he heard this, he was very sorrowful: for he was very rich" (Luke 18:18, 22–23).

Jesus' words to the youth are the only instance recorded of His requiring poverty of His followers. The young man was singled out in this respect. And yet the requirement to "sell all that thou hast" is a universal one. The test given the young man was a fundamental feature of the gospel invitation, for it was aimed precisely at what he valued more than God. He came in pride and turned away in despair.

For the gospel invitation makes absolute claims on the soul. Its truth claims are life claims. All competing interests must yield to the purposes of God. Self-rule must end. It is no wonder that Scripture speaks of the offense of the gospel, a visceral repulsion to God's good news and its messengers. In order to free the soul of sin, the gospel upends the soul's values, and in the struggle the soul becomes an arena where final issues are fought out in earnest. The contention is fierce, and the mind is in fearful disarray.

For a while, that is. Repeated rejections of the gospel become easier as resistance becomes habitual. Insistent appeals are easily brushed aside. Yet the easier is all the more deadly, for to resist the voice of God is to risk despair—a paralysis of will and failing of desire toward heaven's offer of salvation. One fears for the rich young man. To turn from the divine welcome at a critical moment when conditions are most favorable for accepting it bodes ominous for the soul. "Now is the accepted time; behold, now is the day of salvation," writes the apostle (2 Cor. 6:2). The writer of Hebrews urges the same: "To day if ye will hear his voice, harden not your hearts" as did the Israelites in the time of Moses (3:7–8).

The Son of God did not harden His heart toward the undeserving. Like the speculator in real estate and the merchant "seeking goodly pearls" of the parables, He "went and sold all that he had" (Matt. 13:44–46). He asks of those He welcomes no more than He Himself gave.

28

REASSURANCE

The double action of divine grace is to bring down and raise up—to mortify pride and revive from despair. God deals in this way with His own child as with the unbeliever. When from feelings of success and well-being we stumble into pride, we must be brought down. We must be reminded of our unworthiness and helplessness apart from God. When from disappointment with life or with ourselves we drop into sinful despair, we must be raised up. We must be reminded of our worth and of what we have before us to do with the help of God.

When we find a fellow believer in despair, we should remind ourselves that though he has slipped into a sinful condition his low spirits themselves are not sinful. The enemy of his soul has perverted a potentially constructive mood into destructive doubt. We should also remember that God is tenderer in dealing with anguished despair than with pride. To a despondent Jonah He put the question "Doest thou well to be angry?" (Jon. 4:4). To a dejected Peter, who had denied Him, the Lord said, "Simon, son of Jonas, lovest thou me?" (John 21:16). We should not forget that believers who have allowed their depression to become despair are in a weakened state requiring compassionate tact as well as honest directness: "What doest thou here, Elijah?" (1 Kings 19:9).

For many believers the temptation to despair comes in the form of nagging thoughts of past failure. It may be an unintended harm done to another, or even an intended harm that has long been forgiven. It may be a lapse in character that permanently affects the life of another. The poet John Donne put it this way:

> Wilt Thou forgive that sin by which I've won
> Others to sin, and made my sin their door?

It may be a persisting sense of guilt for sin that has long ago been confessed and, according to the promise of God, forgiven and yet is still not forgotten. Donne continues,

> Wilt Thou forgive that sin which I did shun
> A year or two; but wallowed in a score?

Few have sinned more despicably than Joseph's older brothers, conspiring against the seventeen-year-old and selling him into bondage. Years later Joseph, having forgiven them, urges them not to continue in guilty fear and self-condemnation. "Come near to me, I pray you. . . . I am Joseph your brother, whom ye sold into Egypt. Now therefore be not grieved, nor angry with yourselves, that ye sold me hither: for God did send me before you to preserve life" (Gen. 45:4–5). Joseph would not have his brothers live on in self-revulsion and defeat.

An injurious act done inadvertently can shadow a life for years, indeed weigh on a mind for a lifetime. We hear of a driver backing over a child, a child's drowning from a momentary lapse in supervision, a negligent hunting accident taking the life of a friend, a fatal car wreck from a dozing off at the wheel from which only the driver survives. Christians are not exempt from such a happening or from bitterness against themselves and even against God for letting it happen. Whose spirits would not drop precipitously during such a time and remain abysmally low indefinitely? It is hard to imagine emotionally rebounding anytime soon thereafter, or scarcely even ever. Yet even at such times, one's spirits need not decline to despair. Even then there is divine comfort to be received and not spurned by the child of God.

Surely our estimation of personal failures must seem to God almost trivial in view of the cost to Him of our redemption and in view also of the great gulf that separates the best of us from perfection. Our Maker "knoweth our frame; he remembereth that we are dust" (Ps. 103:14). He has warm thoughts for the struggling, defeated Christian and is ready with assurances of His love and strength. To refuse to forgive ourselves for that for which we have been forgiven is understandable when the failure is from a human view egregious and irreversible, but to continue in self-rejection is ultimately an act of spiritual nullification: an unwillingness to receive with thanks the kindness of our Redeemer. The God Who promises to forget our confessed sins and failures would have us forget them too. His strength as well as His example is available to help us do so.

The Christian caught in despair has an affectionate friend in the Savior, Who values his faith and desires to rebuild it. If he doubts his salvation, he must be taken back to the rudiments of it. He must be reminded that in matters of salvation God is concerned with his belief now and he must not obsess over the past—whether he actually dotted all the i's and crossed all the t's at that time in his childhood when he faintly remembers making a "decision." Also, natural remediation has a part to play. He must keep up his spiritual regimen but also, it may be, improve sleep habits, reconnect with friends, and pursue responsibilities.

To feel loved and valued in Christ by a compassionate fellow believer will help the sufferer to realize he is loved and valued by the believer's God. Scripture keeps before us the readiness of our God to heal and restore. "The Lord openeth the eyes of the blind: the Lord raiseth them that are bowed down: the Lord loveth the righteous" (Ps. 146:8). Our loving God excels in what He asks us to do: to "lift up the hands which hang down, and the feeble knees" (Heb. 12:12).

This God sees through the murk and gloom of troubled inner weather. "The darkness and the light are both alike to thee," exclaims the psalmist. Indeed for God "the night shineth as the day" (139:12). Our night is never His night. Yet He takes seriously what shadows our thoughts and helps us pass through the dimness. David declares with assurance, "Thou wilt light my candle: the Lord my God will enlighten my darkness" (Ps. 18:28). The Lord controls the humanly uncontrollable both without and within. "He weigheth the waters by measure," said one who knew well those waters (Job 28:25). Another who had passed through desperate times for many months spoke similarly: "The Lord is upon many waters. . . . The Lord sitteth upon the flood; yea the Lord sitteth King for ever" (Ps. 29:3, 10). The psalmist's words have special weight when we consider that the Israelites were land men, not men of the sea, and the sea for them was a terror. The world of the mind too has its terrors, and the Lord rules over those as well.

In Paul's second letter to Timothy we can hear the voice of a great man in pain, heartsick yet hopeful, deeply disappointed yet joyful in what his life has accomplished through the power of God. He is not dejected. Confined in miserable circumstances, awaiting death, he amazingly calls for his reading materials so his work can continue as long as it can. Demas, his young convert, has forsaken him, "having loved this present world" (4:10). Even more poignantly, "all they which are in Asia be turned away from me" (1:15). His dungeon is cold and damp. Could Timothy bring him his cloak? Minus a statement here or there, the letter would be a document of despair. Yet he finds much to rejoice about and much to affirm. "The Lord knoweth them that are his" (2:19).

Paul asks for Mark, a young man in whom he was once deeply disappointed but who is now "profitable for the ministry" (4:11). Mark may have been the youth who fled naked from the scene of Jesus' arrest. He was certainly the companion who left Paul's traveling party on his first missionary journey. Mark evidently had not despaired in those years since his lapse in spiritual purpose but had allowed God to rebuild his life. We meet the reinstated Mark as the author of the second Gospel.

Relief is always timely for sufferers who wait on the Lord. Such relief is never more urgently needed than by the Christian in low spirits tempted to despair. For assurance that relief will come in due time we have the testimony of the psalmist. "Unless the Lord had been my help, my soul had almost dwelt in silence. When I said, My foot slippeth; thy mercy, O Lord, held me up." Though the psalmist's mind was still in agitation, it was not ungovernably so. "In the multitude of my thoughts within me thy comforts delight my soul" (94:17–19).

For the Christian friend in low spirits and agitation of mind, tempted to despair, we must counsel yieldedness, addressing any sin issues, while urging patience and trust. We will remind him that Scripture has encouragement for him, that "none of them that trust in him shall be desolate" (Ps. 34:22). He has a God "that comforteth those that are cast down" (2 Cor. 7:6). With the apostle he can be "perplexed" while yet "not in despair" (2 Cor. 4:8).

And for ourselves, let us keep this thought in readiness. When we are tempted to think we are without value and our life is to no purpose—that our loving God has fathered a worthless child and framed a pointless life or that we have ill managed irredeemably what has been given us—we must spend some time in quiet conversation with Him and let Him tell us differently. He will assure us that we are indeed ever precious to Him, that dimness of view and subdued spirits are not forever—that "light is sown for the righteous, and gladness for the upright in heart" (Ps. 97:11).

Life's Music

When the burnt offering began, the song of the Lord
began also.

2 Chronicles 29:27

29

THE RHYTHMS OF LIFE: AGAIN

It is neither possible nor desirable to even out the rhythms of life. Emotional unevenness is the pulse of our existence. It is affected by our missteps and by circumstances beyond our control. But ultimately it is due to the way we are made and have to get along in a fallen world.

For believers, more may be said. Our Creator is the God of our moods. He ordains them and sends them for our good as well as for His larger purposes. In her prayer Hannah recognized that "the Lord killeth, and maketh alive: he bringeth down to the grave, and bringeth up," and it was for Hannah an emotional truth as well as a physical fact (1 Sam. 2:6). The Lord had raised her spirits by giving her a son, freeing her from despondency. He will do the same for us, graciously raising or dampening our moods and making them work themselves out productively in His purpose and plan.

These are comforting truths for those who must endure with pain the downside of their emotional lives. They can also be life-animating truths. All suffering is purposive in the life of a Christian and able to produce positive good. To recognize the uses of emotional suffering can help us find special purposes in our pain. We should be able by now to see three.

First, low spirits can be a creative time when much that is positive is going on unnoticed in the mind of the sufferer. It is not the house of mirth but the house of mourning where wisdom is likely to be found, says the wise man of Ecclesiastes 7. Good things come from darkness, says David, referring to his development in the womb through the subtle workmanship of God (Ps. 139:13–16). A developing life as well as a growing body can be a work of divine art, and darkness is ordinarily the condition productive of what is best in us. It is a universal principle that accomplishment is attended with difficulty and pain. "In sorrow thou shalt bring forth" has meaning for us all as well as for Eve (Gen. 3:16).

Second, our emotional fluctuations, whether internally or externally caused, are able to widen our understanding. If it is true that we perceive some things about life and about God and ourselves mainly in our emotional lows—that we are more likely to learn wisdom in the house of mourning—it seems also true that we see other things more clearly when we are on an emotional height. When we are down, we are impressed with the wrongness of our condition in the flesh and in the world and with our unworthiness to be blessed. When we are up, we recognize the rightness of our condition in God—our enviable status as His blessed ones. We catch a glimpse of His ongoing positive purposes in our lives.

During emotional valleys our thoughts are painfully concentrated on what is disappointing in our personal existence—our childlike proneness to missteps and misapprehensions, our weakness of purpose and will, our patterns of failure, our total need for divine guidance and strength. These times may expose particular areas of negligence but will certainly reveal a vast dependency on a strength greater than our own. On the high peaks our thoughts open out upon a reassuring landscape of providential ordering. Positive patterns appear that were hidden before. Whereas we saw more closely and painfully from the depths, we now see more distantly and expectantly—more adequately in a total way—on the heights. The two views, the microscopic and the macroscopic, combine most usefully. Those afflicted with the wider or longer fluctuations suffer more but can see more too.

Not so with those who let their moods decline into pride or despair. The one produces false sight, the other denial that sight is to be had. These can become ingrained spiritual attitudes. "Take heed . . . that the light which is in thee be not darkness," said the Lord to His prideful enemies (Luke 11:35). "Every one that is of the truth heareth my voice," He said to skeptical Pilate, who replied, "What is truth?" (John 18:37–38). Pride and despair, far from enlarging spiritual sight, eclipse it. They deprive their victims of the gains of the mood variations given by God.

Spiritual maturity helps preserve the gains of the emotional crests during the emotional troughs, and also those of the troughs during the crests. It can draw on memory to adjust the extremes toward the center. While down, we can more likely remember what we experienced of God when we were up: His goodness displayed on the broad canvas of our lives and our importance to Him as "His workmanship" (Eph. 2:10). While up, we can more likely remember what gripped us when we were down: our unworthiness of His goodness and our need to do better in areas of weakness and failure. We can blend the insights of the one into those of the other and thus moderate their destabilizing potential. For whereas there is that in us which should give us grief, there is also that in us which should give us delight. The one tempers our elation, the other our depression. This sense of our double status as children of God in a fallen world can encourage and settle us and also motivate us to live godly lives in times of distress (1 Pet. 1:3–9, 13–16).

The patriarch Jacob, who understood more than most will ever know of what life can bring of gains and deprivations, seems able to hold together both awarenesses as he prays to his God just before passing over the brook Jabbok to meet his estranged brother Esau. During his twenty years serving his maternal uncle, Jacob had gained wealth but had also been chastened in character through servile labor to the selfish Laban. In prayer Jacob remembers both the good things he has received from God and also his unworthiness. He is humbly grateful for his blessings from God. He is also terrified. "I am not worthy of the least of all the mercies, and of all the truth, which thou hast shewed unto thy servant; for with my staff I passed over this Jordan; and now I am become two bands. Deliver me, I pray thee, from the hand of my brother, from the hand of Esau: for I fear him, lest he will come and smite me, and the mother with the children" (Gen. 32:10–11).

Jacob's emotional lows, those recorded in Scripture, came in response to circumstances brought upon him largely by his misdoings, but he copes with them here in a way that is exemplary for us all. He is able to incorporate positive insights when his spirits are at their negative pole. Disappointments coupled with successes are deeply impressed on his mind, giving him a wider view of life and a larger view of God. These appear in his maturing responses. Now, preparing to face Esau, fearful Jacob recognizes his blessing by God. Like David he proves able to "bless the Lord at all times" (Ps. 34:1).

Third, our emotional fluctuations can show others more of God, the enabler of our inner life. Christlikeness does not require emotional evenness. It requires spiritual consistency within emotional variation. Scripture shows God in diverse modes: in calm majestic serenity but also in earnest engagement with man, in fearsome indignation but also in tender compassion, in exultation but also in sorrow from refusals of His grace. Yet through all there is continuity. The same divine voice is unmistakable throughout. So it can be with those whom Christ has redeemed and who are being shaped by the Holy Spirit into His image. He can reveal Himself through the ebb and flow of our spirits, indeed quite powerfully through a troubled mind.

In fact, the wider, longer, or more frequent the emotional swings, the more visible whatever spiritual steadiness is there. Greater effort and skill are needed to keep a ship on course during a stormy passage than are required in fair weather and calm seas, and the achievement is comparably more. To hold steady spiritually amidst the tossings of the emotional life without the cargo breaking loose is irresistible evidence of divine strengthening. Especially is it so when the lows are troubling and extreme. It is a truism in the financial world that the wise do not sell their stock in good companies during bad times. To be, like Paul, in distress yet not in despair puts one's faith in bold relief (2 Cor. 4:8). Whether the cause of the distress is outer or inner, an unwavering spiritual rectitude despite it all shows the goodness and greatness of God as little else can.

Jesus bequeathed to His disciples His peace and joy in a time of emotional heaviness, a burdening of the spirit which He felt as well as they. It was for them a time of dreaded deprivation. They would be losing, so they thought, the One Who had led them for three and a half years, in Whom they had put their confidence as the promised divine Messiah. It was for them a time of mourning, and the Lord comforted them with the assurance of a divine continuing presence. His Father would send a Comforter, Who would perform for them the functions for which they had looked to Him (John 14:16–17). In fact, the Father and He Himself would also come (v. 23). God, the entire Godhead, would be a constant comforting presence, a condition superior even to the one they had known these years with Him. They would be steadied with what steadied Him. "Peace I leave with you, my peace I give unto you" (v. 27). "These things have I spoken unto you, that my joy might remain in you, and that your joy might be full" (15:11).

In a messianic passage God through Isaiah had promised these very mind states. "For ye shall go out with joy, and be led forth with peace" (55:12). The Good Shepherd would be leading His small, fearful flock into a threatening world in which wolves disguised as sheep would try to destroy them and hireling shepherds would exploit them. He would go before them, and they would follow with His calmness of mind. His peace and His joy would be for them an abiding possession. For "holy mourning," as Matthew Henry puts it, "is consistent with spiritual joy, and the way to eternal joy. Christ was now troubled, now in sorrow, now in fear, now for a season; but it would not be so always, it would not be so long."[1] The world takes note when a follower of Christ, like the psalmist, can "bless the Lord . . . in all places of his dominion," on the hills and in the valleys of the emotional life (Ps. 103:22).

Psalm 84 speaks of a highway through the valley of Baca, the valley of sorrow. A highway is a road ridged up and leveled so as to afford smooth passage through uneven terrain. Such a throughway does exist for the mood-tossed Christian, a highway to God and with God. It is the way of the Savior's peace and joy.

30

THE RICH VARIETY OF GOD

Our highs and lows then give us useful information about ourselves and about life—and about God. They also allow us to show more of how our Christianity works in a fallen world. Another reason takes us to the purposes of the Creator. Our God loves variety, and this love of variety is reflected in the dissimilarities of His creatures. He created according to "kinds," but within the creaturely kinds as well as amongst them is a fascinating diversity.

This diversity appears notably within humankind. When we meet someone for the first time, physical differences dominate our impressions. Soon we become aware also of distinctive emotional features, and they become part of our sense of that person. We all differ emotionally as well as physically, and someone's emotional makeup is essential in what we refer to as his personality. Could it not be that emotional differences among humans like those between the sexes were in God's mind from the beginning and are intended for good? If so, we should be prepared to find divine purpose in our emotional variability. We recall that all that is natural about us originally is the work of God and that God purposes good in all His work, in creation and redemption.

It is true that capacities for good have a comparable potential for evil. A winsomely extroverted personality can spin giddily out of control, and squander its potential for blessing others. A richly introverted personality can stagnate into morose self-absorption and fail to realize its creative possibilities. In us all, the wear and tear of life itself can level down or pervert unique capacities intended to flourish in the will of God. Special emotional strengths have special vulnerabilities, and Satan knows them well.

It is less obvious that our emotional incapacities have potentialities also for good. Just as there are chronic physical disorders, acquired in life or carried from birth, so are there emotional disorders of long continuance or even perpetual duration. They need not be liabilities. Emotional infirmities, like physical ones, are opportunities for the grace of God to show itself in special ways. They can be understood as endowments for achievement of a high order and as signal evidence of the favor of God. Deficiencies as well as strengths can empower a life for God, Whose "strength is made perfect in weakness" (2 Cor. 12:9).

Evidently God has created emotional differences because He enjoys variety and also because He has different things for His different creatures to do. In the larger order of creation, the species perform their functions in a diverse but blended way for the good of the whole. The term *ecology* would have little meaning did not animals and plants and their surroundings contribute, each in its way, to the common good. Likewise in the Christian world, differences would seem to have practical justifications. The church described in Acts drew from all sectors of society and many nations individuals who would exercise diverse gifts for the benefit of the church and its ministry to the world.

Notice the temperamental differences in the followers of Christ described in the Gospel narratives. There is boisterous Peter but also sensitive John, bustling Martha but also pensive Mary. Diversity existed also within individual disciples, for human natures are too complex to be summed in terms of single traits. So unobtrusive a pair as John and James could also be volatile enough to be nicknamed by the Lord "sons of thunder" (Mark 3:17). The Lord loved them all and valued their natures one and the same. He also refined them. We see Him calming the agitated Martha and speaking supportively of Mary. Years after His return to the Father, we sense in their Epistles a divine mellowing in a tender yet still fervent Peter and in a deeply affectionate yet still animated John.

The Master Himself was seen somewhat variously by different observers. When Jesus asked His twelve disciples "Whom do men say that I the Son of man am?" they replied, "Some say that thou art John the Baptist: some, Elias; and others, Jeremias, or one of the prophets" (Matt. 16:13–14). Certain observers had seen in Him a rugged outwardness of manner that corresponded to their idea of Elijah and to what they had seen in his prophetic counterpart, John the Baptist. Others noted a sensitive inwardness that recalled what they knew from their Scriptures of the poet-prophet Jeremiah. Neither Elijah nor Jeremiah possessed an identity with sufficient breadth to convey the full human personality of the Son of Man seen by the multitudes. The disciples, transformed by the Spirit of God, would reflect the divine Person more entirely as a group than could any one of them alone.

So it is with us. The most widely gifted can show only poorly the rich diversity of the divine personality revealed in the Savior. The best each of us can hope to achieve is a faithful but partial revelation of the Person of our Lord. Together we can more fully show that Person. Whereas individually we are temples of the Holy Spirit, corporately we are the body of Christ. Thus when Jesus prayed that His disciples would "be one," He was praying for their manifestation of His Person corporately just as He had come to manifest the Father in His individual life. By the composite witness of their characters and personalities—their unity within multiplicity—the world would receive a more comprehensive and compelling account of the Person of God.

It follows that we must be prepared to recognize what might be called different styles of spirituality. There is an unfortunate tendency to identify true spirituality with certain personality types. An extrovert may associate vital spirituality with social energy and earnestness—with the Peter or Martha personality. These outgoing types can project a vibrant, dynamic public witness of Spirit-empowered character and can be greatly used of God in an expansive way. A more reticent, reflective Christian may associate spirituality with a richly developed inner life centering on God and with sensitivity to others' needs—with the John or Mary personality. The inward type can be used no less powerfully by God, but likely in a more intensely focused way. Its deep fervencies, like Hannah's, can be easily misjudged (1 Sam. 1:12–14).

Each temperamental type has its strengths and weaknesses, and neither should be valued above the other. Nor should they be seen as mutually exclusive. There will be a devotional core to the most outgoing of spiritual lives and a cordial openness to the most introverted when each has reached maturity in Christ. Even so, natural temperament will have an influence on spiritual manner, and this is good. The work of God would not flourish so well if all dispositions were the same. The buoyant, the reticent, those expert in organization, the masters of devotional thought, those who live in the world without, those who carry their world within—all are needed for God's work today, and all have left their mark in the rich legacy of our faith. But particularly to our point, temperamental differences render more visible the rich variety of God.

Not only in the group but also in the individual life the Creator intends variety. There is divine purpose in it all. Connecting similarities exist among all that God has created, but it is His pleasure never to make any two things exactly the same. In life we never meet exactly the same object or situation twice. What may seem like monotony never quite is. God intends it that way. A life responsive to Him is a tapestry of different threads, dark as well as bright, brief or of some duration, revealing its patterns often only from a distance. Such a life is a narrative of intertwining strands, some of distress and disappointment, others of delight and gratification, the brighter dominating more and more in the emerging pattern. "The path of the just is as the shining light, that shineth more and more unto the perfect day" (Prov. 4:18).

In the emotional life, as in the larger world of His creation, God desires to set against all that is shifting and variable His unchanging perfections and unfailing truth. Amidst the richly diverse yet sometimes painful alternations of our feelings can appear all the more strikingly the beauty of the One in "whom is no variableness, neither shadow of turning" (James 1:17). The variegated life He ordains for us sets off beautifully the constancy of His faithfulness and love.

I have associated what I have called the rhythms of life with the flow of music. Music of the highest order has like life its regularities—its patterns and themes. It has also its surprises, its departures from pattern; for it plays on expectations, sometimes appearing to frustrate them before resolving them. Even within the pattern itself can be contrasting elements that seem to jar. Some of the most gorgeous music ever composed, Bach's for example, incorporates dissonance as well as passages in a minor mode.

It is no less true in the divine harmonics of a dedicated life that pain may intrude unexpectedly or return at feared intervals in a disturbing way. Dark overtones may dominate at times and seem to shadow the whole until all is resolved and the Composer's work is done. The somber strands are part of the divine masterwork. It would be lesser without them. The descent from elation to depression is never a welcome one, to be sure, but both meet artfully in the richest music of life.

Epilogue

Substance is in them, when they cast their leaves.

Isaiah 6:13

EPILOGUE

JACOB'S TWO PILLARS

The patriarch Jacob knew recurring trouble in his long life, much of it traceable to his own poor judgment. Yet trouble was not the whole of it. There were those wonderful moments when God came to him to encourage and bless him. Jacob evidently had persistent doubts about the reality of the blessing he had obtained from his father by trickery. God reassured him repeatedly at critical times that he was indeed heir to the blessing given to his grandfather Abraham and his father, Isaac, and that he indeed remained within His special care. Jacob's life as recorded in Scripture was a succession of delights and disappointments and may well picture for us the peaks and valleys of our emotional lives.

One of the major moments in Jacob's life occurred on his return from his twenty years serving his uncle Laban, during which he had acquired his two wives and amassed considerable wealth. He entered Canaan from the east, settling briefly at Shechem, as had his grandfather Abraham years before. There his daughter Dinah was violated by the prince of the town, and two of her brothers retaliated by slaughtering all the males. Jacob, disheartened, was then instructed by God to remove to Bethel, where he had first met

God in a dream, and to build an altar there. He had his family and servants put away their false gods and associated objects, which he buried under an oak in Shechem, and then came to Bethel. There God appeared to him again, repeating the patriarchal blessing and again declaring his name to be Israel.

It was a high moment in Jacob's life. One can hardly imagine a more exhilarating experience. Jacob marked it with a visible memorial. "And Jacob set up a pillar in the place where [God] talked with him, even a pillar of stone" (Gen. 35:14). It was the second time God had met him there, and he named it again Bethel, the house of God. Jacob would remember it as "the place where God spake with him" and reassured him that His promises for Jacob held firm.

Jacob evidently did not stay there long. Nor would his spirits. After leaving Bethel, when "there was but a little way to come to Ephrath," his beloved Rachel went into "hard labour" and died in childbirth (35:16). The child lived and was named by his dying mother Benoni, "son of my sorrow." Jacob, however, called him Benjamin, "son of my right hand" (3:18). The father, having himself been renamed more positively (from supplanter to prince with God), renamed more positively his son. The narrative closes with poignant brevity. "Rachel died, and was buried in the way to Ephrath, which is Bethlehem. And Jacob set a pillar upon her grave: that is the pillar of Rachel's grave unto this day" (35:19–20).

The two pillars can speak to us of the rhythms of life. Not infrequently from those emotional heights when it seems nothing can ever draw us down again to despondency it is "but a little way to come to Ephrath." We descend to the very depths of our desires and hopes, whence it seems nothing can raise us ever again to happiness of heart. But there is something in a detail of this story that may soften the sorrow.

Jacob dealt with the loss of his wife by calling her child a special son, the "son of my right hand." The right hand signified pre-eminence in privilege and honor. We may recall another couple nearing Ephrath almost two millennia later with the woman in labor who would give to the world a special child. It was a child promised to give her sorrow—"A sword shall pierce through thine own soul also," said old Simeon. But the sorrow was not all. He would be the Son of His Father's right hand. He Himself would be "a man of sorrows, and acquainted with grief," but He would be also the great Redeemer from the right hand of His Father. From Ephratah came Calvary, and because of Calvary we "sorrow not, even as others which have no hope" (1 Thess. 4:13). The lesson of Jacob's two pillars is that sublimity and sorrow belong to our lives but not in pointless succession. There is purpose in it all.

The loss of Rachel was not the last of Jacob's sorrows. More disappointments would follow, some that would shake him to the foundation stones of his life. But when we trace them to the end, we find the pillars reversing order. Jacob would be reunited with his lost son. When Jacob was leaving the land promised to him and his descendants for Egypt to meet Joseph, God met him "in visions of the night" and reassured him once again. "I will go down with thee into Egypt; and I will also surely bring thee up again" (Gen. 46:4). So would He also later with the father of a promised Child fleeing the threat of Herod.

Jacob's Great Companion is ours also. In the troughs and crests of our emotional lives His presence is constant. He goes down with us and brings us up again. He steers us through rough seas He wills not to calm. He eases losses He chooses not to remove and counters them with gains. He takes notice of the pillars we raise to sanctify the highs and lows of our lives.

NOTES

Chapter 1

1. *As You Like It*, 2.1.12, *Riverside Shakespeare*, 2nd ed. (Boston: Houghton, 1997); all citations will refer to this edition.

2. *Richard II*, 2.1.8.

Chapter 5

1. *On Religious Affections in Works* (1834; rpt., Peabody, MA: Hendrickson, 2000), 238.

Chapter 9

1. *Studies in the Prophecy of Jeremiah* (Westwood, NJ: Revell, 1931), 35.

Chapter 10

1. *Institutes of the Christian Religion*, trans. Henry Beveridge (Grand Rapids, MI: Eerdmans, 1989), III.x.33–34.

2. *Studies in the Prophecy of Jeremiah* (Westwood, NJ: Revell, 1931), 33.

Chapter 12

1. *A Midsummer Night's Dream* 1.1.134.

Chapter 17

1. *The Gospel of Matthew* (Westwood, NJ: Revell, 1929), 93.

Chapter 20

1. *Matthew Henry's Commentaries.* vol. 6, 459.

2. *The Dedicated Life: Studies in Romans* (rpt., Belfast: Ambassador, 1997).

Chapter 23

1. Letter to Princess Elizabeth of Denmark, May 31, 1643, quoted in Samuel Stumpf, *Philosophical Problems*, 4th ed. (New York: McGraw-Hill, 1994), 330.

2. Dublin: Curry, 1843.

3. "The Creative Brain," in *Classical, Renaissance, and Postmodernist Acts of the Imagination*, ed. Arthur F. Kinney (Newark: U of Delaware P, 1996), 285.

Chapter 25

1. *Thoughts for Sundays* (Chattanooga, TN: AMG, 1969), 146.

Chapter 26

1. Harold Skulsky, "Despair," *Spenser Encyclopedia*, (Toronto: Toronto UP, 1990).

Chapter 29

1. *Matthew Henry's Commentaries.* vol. 6, 1078.